a Malawi
ate Professor of Black Literature at
the U̶͟͟͟͟͟͟ of N̶͟͟͟͟ O̶͟͟͟͟͟ in the USA. He has also
taugh͟͟͟͟͟ College in
North͟͟͟͟ iversity of
Zamb͟͟͟͟ American
Litera͟͟͟͟ and Yale
unive͟͟͟͟ *Reflections*
(NEC͟͟͟͟ sh by a
Mala͟͟͟͟ *it for Me*
(Rava͟͟͟͟ Honour-
able ͟͟͟͟ the 1985 Noma Award for Publishing in Africa,
Nightwatcher, Nightsong (Paul Green, Peterborough, 1986), and
Whispers in the Wings (Heinemann, Oxford, 1991). He is also the
editor of *When My Brothers Come Home: Poems from Central and
Southern Africa* (Wesleyan University Press, Middletown, Connec-
ticut, 1985), a major regional anthology cited on the Kwanzaa
Honours List (1987) by Dennis Brutus. He is widely published in
journals and anthologies in Africa, the USA, Canada, Europe and
India. His novel, *In A Dark Season*, written in the 1970s, will soon
be published in the Heinemann African Writers Series.

STELLA P. CHIPASULA was educated at Lilongwe Girls'
Secondary School and Providence Teachers' College in Mulanje,
and taught in Malawian and Zambian primary schools for several
years. She resumed her education in the USA, first at Albertus
Magnus College in New Haven, Connecticut, then at the Univer-
sity of Rhode Island in Providence, St Olaf College in Northfield,
Minnesota, and finally at the University of Nebraska at Omaha,
where she graduated with a BA in Art History. She has written
some poems, worked on Malawian folktales, and is currently
writing a romance for Heinemann's Heartbeat Series. She works
in the Reference Section of the Library at the University of
Nebraska at Omaha.

THE HEINEMANN BOOK OF AFRICAN WOMEN'S POETRY

Edited by Stella and Frank Chipasula

Heinemann

Heinemann Ecucational Publishers
Halley Court, Jordan Hill, Oxford OX2 8EJ
A part of Harcourt Education Limited

Heinemann is the registered trademark of
Harcourt Education Limited

Introduction, selection and notes
© Stella and Frank Chipasula 1995

First published by Heinemann Educational Publishers in 1995

British Library Cataloguing in Publication Data
A Catalogue record for this book is available from the British Library.

AFRICAN WRITERS SERIES and CARIBBEAN WRITERS SERIES
and their accompanying logos are trademarks in the
United States of America of Heinemann:
A Division of Reed Publishing (USA) Inc.

Cover design by Stafford & Stafford
Cover illustration by Hassan Aliyu

10-digit ISBN: 0 435906 80 1
13-digit ISBN: 978 0 435906 80 1

Phototypeset by Wilmaset Ltd, Birkenhead, Wirral

Printed and bound in India by Multivista Global Limited

CONTENTS

GHANA

NIGERIA

ZIMBABWE

for
Helen, *Bringer of light*
Eunice, Ida and Dina (in memoriam)
Our mothers
Theodora, Barbara & Sherry
Their daughters

I am life. I am strength. I am woman.
Julia de Burgos

*Does there exist, as a subterranean current
below the surface structure of male-oriented
language, a specifically female language, a
'mother tongue'?*
Alicia Ostriker

PREFACE

In their introduction to *The Penguin Book of Modern African Poetry*, the editors wrote that the almost exclusively male poets they had 'discovered' and added to their pioneering book had 'extended the range of African poetry in many directions'. Yet they hadn't taken account of the missing dimension of women's poetry. The main purpose of this anthology is to redress the balance, bringing to light at least some of the abundant good poetry by women in Africa which is so conspicuously absent from other collections.

Although for many years both male and female critics have analysed images of women in African male poets' works, they have paid hardly any attention to women's own self-portraiture. Studies of Negritude poetry, for instance, abound with discussions of the portrayal of the black woman as a symbol of beauty, maternal warmth, nurture, and Mother Africa. Through their own poetry, however, African women redefine and re-present themselves in their own terms and offer us rare insights into their inner lives and experiences.

This book's exclusive focus on women's poetry is a necessary first step towards reversing the objectification of women and rendering visible the invisible poets themselves. We hope that as a result of this anthology's publication, future anthologies of African poetry will ensure equitable representation of all serious poets regardless of sex and race. As this anthology becomes well known we hope it will mother other anthologies that will fill the gaps that this one could not, in order to enlarge the picture of African poetry.

We have benefited from the efforts of several scholars and translators who deserve special mention. Dr Jacques-Noël Gouat and Professor Eric Sellin of Tulane University translated a significant number of the poems from the French, while Julia Kirst translated some from the Portuguese. We received a great deal of support from many of the women poets themselves and also from Sherry O'Brien and Christine Erickson, who read early versions of the book and made very useful comments. More encouragement came in the form of a Faculty Development Grant from St Olaf College which facilitated the completion of the initial version of the anthology. For considering the project worthy of the award, we wish to express our gratitude to the Committee.

Finally, we would like Helen to know that she brought into our lives the new light of inspiration that renewed our faith in the viability of the work. And to Masauko we offer the following advice: *listen hard to your mother's songs; from them you might learn a lot about yourself.*

This book was willed by all the women poets represented in it; they are the true owners of this anthology.

Frank and Stella Chipasula, 1995

INTRODUCTION

This anthology breaks new ground in African poetry, where women poets have been marginalised and neglected. Under-representation of women poets in existing anthologies means that the present book fills a real and perceivable gap in African letters. We hope to inspire women to reclaim their historic role as singers of the songs that constituted a major part of our poetic experience during childhood. Our purpose is to celebrate African women's poetry as a repository of essential cultural and spiritual values that continue to shape our lives.

Conceived as a gathering of African women's voices, this book remaps Africa's vast poetic landscape, celebrating the racial and cultural unity-in-diversity of the African continent and its islands. Further, it goes against the grain of traditional scholarship which tends to isolate the northern regions. Covering practically the whole African continent, the anthology reintegrates the Islamic Arab North and Egypt into the rest of the continent as a way of fostering solidarity among the diverse cultures.

The earliest poem in the book was composed by Queen Hatshepsut (also called Hashepsowe), who reigned as a male pharaoh in the Eighteenth Dynasty, at the peak of Egypt's power. This long poetic obelisk inscription, which survives today, was left among her inscriptions on tombs in her magnificent mortuary and funerary temple at Deir el Bahri. The poem reveals Hatshepsut's power and grandeur, which she attributes to her father, Amun, to whom she built one of the monuments. Curiously, though, the inscription makes no mention of her mother.

A more modern monumental work in the women's poetic tradition, which shares with the communally performed oral poetry the function of transmitting cultural values from one generation to another, appears here as a fragment. In 1858, in anticipation of her impending death, Mwana Kupona binti Msham, a Swahili woman, wrote her famous *Utendi wa Mwana Kupona* ('Mwana Kupona's Poem') for the instruction of her daughter, Mwana Hashima binti Sheik. Though overtly didactic, the poem nevertheless reveals the intensity of a mother's love and concern for her daughter's well-being, educating the young woman in etiquette and ethics. This carefully structured poem, which runs into about forty *tendi* verses, demonstrates that in Swahili society women have traditionally been custodians of poetry, and that some of the best poetry in the language has been written by them.

Among contemporary women poets, poetry continues to play both functional and aesthetic roles, as even a cursory reading of Noémia de Sousa and Alda do Espirito Santo's work indicates. De Sousa, the first African woman to achieve an international reputation as a poet, played a leading role in the Negritude and protest movements among the painters, poets and writers who spearheaded the cultural renaissance in Maputo, Mozambique, during the 1940s and 1950s. She progressed from being a Negritude poet with such poems as 'If You Want to Know Me' and 'Sangue Negro' to being an unflinchingly defiant protest poet in 'Our Voice', and 'The Poem of João'. In 'Call', de Sousa makes a double call of defiance against colonial and male African oppression as she depicts a village female charcoal seller who is used by her own men as a mere baby factory and is reduced to poverty by the colonial economy. This 'bush' woman who has been announcing her wares in a 'strangled' and 'tired voice' is simultaneously 'leashed (like a donkey) with children' by her husband and psychologically lashed into submission by the colonial authority. Thus the disadvantages of gender, race and class constitute a triple yoke that grips the Mozambican peasant woman. Sexually exploited by her own men, she has also been scarred by the 'mean and brutal rhino-whip' of the colonial administrator.

De Sousa's once powerful voice has been silenced by neglect, as has that of Alda do Espirito Santo, from the plantation island of São Tomé, whose verses were once considered subversive and dangerous by the Portuguese colonial authorities. Her work shows that the major concerns of African women poets during colonial rule do not differ from those of their male counterparts. African women poets are as concerned as the men about colonial oppression, and very often their denunciation of colonial atrocities is more ardent and passionate than the male poets'. After the massacre of innocent civilians by the Portuguese army and bands of white settlers on São Tomé from the third to the fifth of February 1953, for instance, do Espirito Santo published such protest poems as 'Where are the Men Chased Away by that Mad Wind?' and others which prompted the Portuguese authorities to arrest and detain her without trial. While in prison do Espirito Santo was tortured but she remained resolute and unbroken and, upon her release, she continued to participate in the anti-colonial struggle and to demand justice for her people.

Although most of her poems remain untranslated, the few samples that are available in English show her strong sympathies for the underdog. Many of her poems deal with the plight of the common workers such as washer women, maids working in white poeple's kitchens, plantation labourers, dock workers, and slum dwellers. Her identification with their suffering is almost total, a fact which may explain her inclusion in *The Penguin Book of Socialist Verse* (ed. Alan Bold. Penguin, Harmondsworth, 1970). The exploitation of African labour by colonial masters, a theme which animates such Angolan male poets as Viriato da Cruz, Antonio Jacinto and Agostinho Neto, finds expression in many of her poems which portray Africans brutalised by hard forced labour on the Portuguese coffee plantations on São Tomé e Príncipe islands.

The theme of male tyranny is treated in the poem 'Arise to the Day's Toil' by Assumpta Acam-Oturu, where the exploitation and abuse of women assumes a never-ending cyclic pattern so that women become permanently enslaved to men's desires. The woman in the poem is constantly ordered about by her husband, implicitly in the language of his former colonial master, which he has apparently internalised to the exclusion of the language of love and tenderness.

Other women have also treated the same theme, most notably Mrs Elimu Njau (as Marina Gashe) in her poem 'The Village', which depicts a 'village of toil' occupied almost exclusively by women since the men have apparently deserted it for a mysterious other world. In this village of missing men, old and young women saddled with the double burden of motherhood and womanhood stir the soil 'like chicken looking for worms', trying to eke out a living on the land. The poem links them metaphorically to the donkey, the ultimate beast of burden.

Great socio-political upheavals have also been occasions for the flowering of poetry in many African countries. With the beginning of the armed struggle against French colonial rule in Algeria in 1954 was born a poetry of combat. Among the intellectuals imprisoned by the French colonial authorities was a group of young women who wrote defiant poetry in prison. Anna Gréki and Malika O'Lahsen were among those who turned from purely anti-colonial poetry that listed colonial abuses to a poetry that validated the armed struggle as a viable means of liberating the country.

Anna Gréki's poems, interspaced with evocations of her child-hood in the Aures Mountains, are expressions of solidarity and sisterhood with the fighting women who ran guns and messages during the war. Like her compatriots, she is not content to recount her personal nightmares but she consciously wishes to raise the morale of her sisters in the struggle. 'The future is soon', she declares with certainty in one poem, in order to fortify the fighters' determination to restore their ravaged nation. Through the simile of the 'walls closed like fists' she links the prison walls with the 'clenched fists' of those struggling outside, and fuses the struggles into one. Prison poetry thus transformed into combat poetry plays a double role of exposing colonial atrocities and projecting the poet-fighters' vision of a liberated Algeria. The 'builders of liberty and tenderness' are both the sisters and brothers fighting outside and those unbowed by incarceration. They are united in the common struggle to reclaim the land and to restore justice and love.

The magnitude of male oppression is clearly articulated in Leila Djabali's poem, 'For my Torturer, Lieutenant D . . .' in which she recreates the proceedings in a torture chamber, the all-night electric shocks and beatings, in such harrowing images as 'a locomotive in my belly' and 'rainbows before my eyes'. And then as she interrogates this man, we realise that his heart has hardened into stone. This experience is not isolated; Djabali's voice echoes other muted women's voices all over Africa.

In South Africa, women's awareness of poetry as a weapon against apartheid energises their work. In the poems of Lindiwe Mabuza, Amelia Pegram and Ingrid Jonker, for instance, we encounter not only the unveiled spectre of apartheid but also articulate voices of combatants for equality, freedom and justice. Celebrations of heroes fallen on battlefields and in prisons, deaths in the mines, exile – these are the preoccupations of the political poets; they are interwoven in this anthology with poems addressing wide-ranging human concerns such as love, motherhood, death, and the quest for self-assured womanhood and human dignity.

African women poets are engaged in a double struggle out of invisibility and silence, one part of which is the search for a healing and life-giving language. The most articulate of them draw upon the stylistic elements of oral poetry in order to root their works in their cultures. Many of these, particularly Noémia de Sousa, Alda do Espirito Santo, Rashidah Ismaili Abubakr and Ama Ata Aidoo, adopt conversational and song styles as well as techniques from folk poetry in a conscious attempt to reconnect themselves to the continuum of literary performance and living traditions. In some cases, the poets have successfully recovered and renewed long-dead forms. The experiments of the South African poet, Jeni Couzyn, who has composed modern spells, are examples of her laudable effort at reclaiming an ancient and universal genre found in the Egyptian *Book of the Dead*.

This anthology integrates poetry originally written in English with that translated from the French, Portuguese and Afrikaans. Despite the difficulties and losses that result from translation, a great deal of the cultural values are carried over from the original languages into English. We have simply attempted to set in motion a cross-cultural dialogue among the various voices represented here. Such a gathering, covering practically the whole of continental Africa and its islands, enables the reader to appreciate the parallels and affinities that exist among the mother tongues of African peoples.

This is the only anthology of African women poets in existence to date. While a few African women poets have been included in such international anthologies as Aliki and Willis Barnstone's *Women Poets of the World from Antiquity to Now* (Schocken Books, New York, 1978), *The Penguin Book of Women Poets* (eds Carol Cosman, Joan Keefe and Kathleen Weaver. Penguin, New York, 1978), *Women Poets of the World* (eds Joanna Bankier, Deirdre Lashgari and Doris Earnshaw. Macmillan, New York, 1983), and *The Other Voice: Twentieth-Century Women's Poetry in Translation* (ed. Joanna Bankier. Norton, New York, 1976), no single volume devoted exclusively to their work has hitherto been published. The under-representation of women poets in anthologies is traceable to Léopold Sédar Senghor's landmark *Antologie de la Nouvelle Poésie Nègre et Malgache de la Langue Française* (1948), and the general under-estimation of women's poetry is reflected in the few women poets included in anthologies thereafter. For instance, when Gerald Moore and Ulli Beier first published their *Modern Poetry From Africa* in 1963, they included only Noémia de Sousa and Alda do Espirito Santo although such poets as Gladys May Casely Hayford (alias Aqua Lalua), Mabel Segun, Alda Lara, Maria Eugénia Lima and Yetunde Pereira had published their work in Africa, Brazil, the United States, England and Portugal, by that time.

With the transformation of the Moore-Beier anthology into the now classic *Penguin Book of Modern African Poetry*, as it entered its third edition, only one other woman poet, Molara Ogundipe-Leslie, has found her place among its pages. The editors misrepresent Alda do Espirito Santo as a man (Ald*o*), an error which is repeated in *300 Years of Black Poetry* (1970) edited by Alan Lomax and Raoul Abdul, and in Alan Bold's anthology, *The Penguin Book of Socialist Verse*.

Superficially, these misrepresentations may appear to have very little or no significance, but they may have been responsible for creating the impression that there were no women poets worth serious attention in Africa. Instead of redoubling their efforts at locating women poets for inclusion in their anthologies, later editors may have been convinced about the futility of such an exercise.

An examination of later poetry anthologies reveals a trend that continues to favour male poets at the expense of women. Out of 50 poets in David Cook and David Rubadiri's *Poems from East Africa* (1971), for example, only six are women. This is a fair representation considering that in John Reed and Clive Wake's *French African Verse with English Translations* (1972), only one woman, Anoma Kanie from the Ivory Coast, is represented by two poems, both dated 1952, from her own poetry volume, *Les eaux du Camoe* (1952). A great stride, if we recall that in 1965 Clive Wake included no women in his own *An Anthology of African and Malagasy Poetry*. Even *An Introduction to East African Poetry* (1976), co-edited by Jonathan Kariara and Ellen Kitonga, has only four women out of 23 poets. And although Angola has many women poets, only one woman (Deolinda Rodrigues) appears in Michael Wolfers' *Poems from Angola* (1979), which gathers the works of 22 poets. By far the most important omission occurs in Isidore Okpewho's *The Heritage of African Poetry* (1985), which, designed as a teaching anthology, certainly perpetuates the male 'heritage' of African poetry. Perhaps the only anthology to have devoted a fair amount of space to women poets is Jack Cope and Uys Krige's *The Penguin Book of South African Verse* (1968), which contains 16 women out of 66 poets.

African women poets have also been excluded from the published literary histories. To date, only a handful of women poets appear in these histories; in a few cases, poets who happen to have been mentioned in an early edition of a book are inexplicably dropped from a later one. For instance, in his *Muntu: The New African Culture* (1958), Janheinz Jahn cites Aldo (sic) do Espirito Santo as one of the two major poets from São Tomé, and Noémia de Sousa as the sole poet of Mozambique! Curiously, though, these two poets do not reappear in his *Neo-African Literature: A History of Black Writing* (1966), although he mentions Gladys May Casely Hayford as a 'conformist', among the three prominent Ghanaian poets.

If the literary histories are disappointing as sources, bibliographies and author guides are even more so. Out of the 292 poets recorded by Donald Herdeck in his *African Authors: A Companion to*

Black African Writing: Vol. I: 1300–1973 (1973), only 13 are women. The *New Readers Guide to African Literature* has included profiles of African women writers, but it still lacks information on women poets. However, the picture has begun to change with the publication of Brenda Berrian's invaluable *Bibliography of African Women Writers and Journalists* (1985), and Christine Guyonneau's 'Francophone Women Writers from Sub-Saharan Africa' (*Callaloo* Number 24, Spring–Summer 1985), which list women poets as well.

The current anthology seeks to complete the picture of African poetry in order to enlarge the field of African literature as a whole. As a pioneering work, this anthology excavates and exposes a wealth of material that has lain forgotten in numerous obscure places. We claim no expertise in this enterprise; we have merely undertaken the spade-work of laying bare the unmined wealth of African women's poetry. As long as the women poets are denied their voices, no meaningful discussion of African literary art is complete. Our aim is to reintegrate our *first* singers into the mainstream and forefront of African literature where they right-fully belong. This is the time to re-member our mothers' severed tongues, and to remember their voices and bittersweet songs.

North Africa
Algeria
Egypt
Morocco
Tunisia

Danièle Amrane

You Called to Me, Prison Windows

I am afraid of the unknown
And yet I walked toward it when I went away from here
And that is when I saw you
You called out to me
Prison windows
Barred windows
And behind the bars
You my brothers
Behind the bars
Straight and cold
An ocean of life
And in my name
Which you shouted
A message of love
I took with me your image
Your faces full of laughter
Your faces full of life
Behind those black bars
And I no longer feel I have the right to be sad
I don't know you
And perhaps I never will
But I love you
As I love
The minarets of Tlemcen
I love you
As I love
The paths in the Kabyle mountains
I love you
But I do not know how to sing my love

Translated from the French by Eric Sellin

Leila Djabali

For my Torturer, Lieutenant D . . .

You slapped me –
  no one had ever slapped me –
electric shock
and then your fist
and your filthy language
I bled too much to be able to blush
All night long
a locomotive in my belly
rainbows before my eyes
It was as if I were eating my mouth
drowning my eyes
I had hands all over me
and felt like smiling.

Then one morning a different soldier came
You were as alike as two drops of blood.
Your wife, Lieutenant –
Did she stir the sugar in your coffee?
Did your mother dare to tell you you looked well?
Did you run your fingers through your kids' hair?

Translated from the French by Anita Barrows

Anna Gréki

Before your Waking

for Ahmad Inal

Before your waking I only knew
How to limit my sight to my eyes' boundary
My eyes could not see past what they remembered

I slept in beds the shape of my bones
And in the barrenness I named sleep
Night's waters and day's eroded one shore

The earth around me quivered like mercury
And if by chance I dreamed of the sun
Its light was torn from me; I was condemned

My suitcase was stuffed with its worldwide tours; but
My life had a little window on the courtyard
You could say that I lodged inside my brain

And nothing anyone said made sense
I called a stubborn desert wisdom
And had no desires except to lament them

The bodies I touched deserted my hands
My movements were plotted by puppet strings
That I called Passion, that I called Reason

Old age was gaining time on me
I'd even forgotten what you say to a child
Who wakes, frightened, and won't let go of your hand;
If I lived at all, it was just out of habit.

Yet even somewhere at the core of this deathly
Solitude – even then – I knew you would come
I knew I was travelling toward my youth

Youth was a mandate, pronounced by your heart's
Rhythm – The future was launched in your arms
I heard it approach without knowing your step

It speaks with the strength and warmth of your courage
And that shame, to say what others keep silent
For foolishness, often, or want of faith

Now I walk hand-in-hand with the earth; and he
Who holds me today will in the end
Love me in another's body.

Translated from the French by Anita Barrows

'The Future is for Tomorrow'

The future is for tomorrow
The future is soon

Beyond the walls closed like clenched fists
Through the bars encircling the sun
Our thoughts are vertical and our hopes
The future coiled in the heart climbs towards the sky
Like upraised arms in a sign of farewell
Arms upright, rooted in the light
In a sign of an appeal to love
To return to my life
I press you against my breast my sister
Builder of liberty and tenderness
And I say to you await tomorrow
For we know

The future is soon
The future is for tomorrow.

Translated from the French by Mildred P. Mortimer

Malika O'Lahsen

It Took One Hundred Years

They are cutting up into pieces
My body and my sun
They are cutting them up into pieces
You
  You will be white
You
  You will be black
Hunger
  Laziness
    Unwillingness

It took
    One hundred years
To make me a savage
It took
    One hundred years
Even more

They are cutting everything up into pieces
Departments
Districts
They are clipping out pictures
With border barbed wire
They are cutting up my body
To make it into History

The Dead Erect

My country is an asylum where madmen
Speak with their eyes
Because they are tongueless
I have walked it
    during the black night
I have walked it
    all the way to silence
I have walked it
    all the way to the grave
I have seen the woods speak
Cities with cold lights
Autos on the sidewalks
Beware
    the sea stifles my sun
Beware
    the sea covers my voice
Today
The madwomen   talk to the rocks
And tell stories to the mountains

Our dead have gone out erect
Our dead left on foot

Translated from the French by Eric Sellin

Queen Hatshepsut

Obelisk Inscriptions

I have done this with a loving heart for my father Amun;
Initiated in his secret of the beginning,
Acquainted with his beneficent might,
I did not forget whatever he had ordained.
My majesty knows his divinity,
I acted under his command;
It was he who led me,
I did not plan a work without his doing.
   It was he who gave directions,
I did not sleep because of his temple,
I did not stray from what he commanded.
My heart was Sia before my father,
I entered into the plans of his heart.
I did not turn my back to the city of the All-Lord,
Rather did I turn my face to it.
I know that Ipet-sut is the lightland on earth,
The august hill of the beginning,
The Sacred Eye of the All-Lord,
His favoured place that bears his beauty,
That gathers in his followers.

It is the King himself who says:
I declare before the folk who shall be in the future,
Who shall observe the monument I made for my father,
Who shall speak in discussion,
Who shall look to posterity –
It was when I sat in the palace,
And thought of my maker,
   That my heart led me to make for him
Two obelisks of electrum,
Whose summits would reach the heavens,
In the august hall of columns,

Between the two great portals of the King,
The Strong Bull, King Aakheperkare, the Horus triumphant.
Now my heart turns to and fro,
In thinking what will the people say,
They who shall see my monument in after years,
And shall speak of what I have done.
Beware of saying, 'I know not, I know not:
Why has it been done?
To fashion a mountain of gold throughout,
Like something that just happened.'
I swear, as I am loved of Re,
As Amun, my father, favours me,
As my nostrils are refreshed with life and dominion,
As I wear the white crown,
As I appear with the red crown,
As the Two Lords have joined their portions for me,
As I rule this land like the son of Isis,
As I am mighty like the son of Nut,
As Re rests in the evening bark,
As he prevails in the morning bark,
As he joins his two mothers in the god's ship,
As sky endures, as his creation lasts,
As I shall be eternal like an undying star,
As I shall rest in life like Atum –
So as regards these two great obelisks,
Wrought with electrum by my majesty for my father Amun,
In order that my name may endure in this temple,
For eternity and everlastingness,
They are each of one block of hard granite,
Without seam, without joining together!

My majesty began work on them in the year 15, second month
of winter, day 1, ending in year 16, fourth month of summer, last
day, totalling seven months of quarry work. I did it for him out of
affection, as a king for a god. It was my wish to make them for him
gilded with electrum. 'Their foil lies on their body', is what I
expect people to say. My mouth is effective in its speech; I do not

go back on my word. Hear ye! I gave for them the finest electrum.
I measured it by the gallon like sacks of grain. My majesty
summoned a quantity beyond what the Two Lands had yet seen.
The ignorant and the wise know it.

Not shall he who hears it say,
'It is a boast', what I have said;
Rather say, 'How like her it is,
She is devoted to her father!'

Lo, the god knows me well,
Amun, Lord of Thrones-of-the-Two-Lands;
He made me rule Black Land and Red Land as reward,
No one rebels against me in all lands.
All foreign lands are my subjects,
He placed my border at the limits of heaven,
What Aten encircles labours for me.
He gave it to him who came from him,
Knowing I would rule it for him.
I am his daughter in very truth,
Who serves him, who knows what he ordains.
My reward from my father is life-stability-rule,
On the Horus throne of all the living, eternally like Re.

Andrée Chedid

The Future and the Ancestor

The dead's right grain
is woven in our flesh
within the channels of the blood
Sometimes we bend
beneath the fullness of ancestors

But the present that shatters walls,
banishes boundaries
and invents the road to come,
rings on.

Right in the centre of our lives
liberty shines,
begets our race
and sows the salt of words.

Let the memory of blood
be vigilant but never void the day.
Let us precede ourselves
across new thresholds.

Translated from the French by Samuel Hazo and Mirène Ghossein

What are We Playing at?

What else can we do
but garden our shadows
while far away
the universe burns and vanishes?

What else can we do
but visit with time
while nearby
time times us to death?

What else can we do
but stop at the horizon
while far away
and nearby –
   the real collision.

Translated from the French by Samuel Hazo and Mirène Ghossein

Man–today

Man is shut in
Man exceeds
               Man retains the bygone
Man detains the to-come.
The fire which gave birth to language
Consumes him
Edifies him.
Man breaks and traps himself
Man assaults the universe
Man is this man
Man is all man
Man–today.

Translated from the French by Samuel Hazo and Mirène Ghossein

Movement

Forge the contrary of this world
Where the soul loses rumours
Where time dries us up
Man perishes from his own poison
But rises in the light he sketches
Give birth to yourself
Cross over yourself
Unite the movement
Stir up that word
Which does not turn away from men
But shapes itself towards them.

Translated from the French by Samuel Hazo and Mirène Ghossein

Imagine

Imagine the ocean
dry as lavender.
Imagine branches
ceasing to be perches
for the birds.
And then on the horizon
imagine death
in its pallor of pallors
letting the dead
live again.

Translated from the French by Samuel Hazo and Mirène Ghossein

Who Remains Standing?

First,
erase your name,
unravel your years,
destroy your surroundings,
uproot what you seem,
and who remains standing?
Then,
rewrite your name,
restore your age,
rebuild your house,
pursue your path,
and then,
endlessly,
start over, all over again.

Translated from the French by Samuel Hazo and Mirène Ghossein

The Naked Face

Faces of the counted years,
but still of such enigmas,

faces without rumours,
faces in expectancy,
faces in constant birth.
Faces of so many cells,

faces that are as you are
and already are not.

Never shall pulses stop
beneath your surfaces,
nor shall my thirst to understand you cease,

you,
one face beneath them all,
naked.

Translated from the French by Samuel Hazo and Mirène Ghossein

For Survival

You shall have, for survival,
Hills of tenderness
The ships of an otherwhere
The delta of love

You shall have, for survival,
The sun of a palm
The draft of a word
The water of the everyday

You shall arrange, for survival,
Braziers   terraces
You'll name the leaf
That enlivens the rock

You shall sing the men
Transfixed by one same breath
Who facing down the mortal shining
Bring their thought to light!

Translated from the French by Marie Ponsot

Stepping Aside

Often   I inhabit my body
as far as the cavities of my armpits
I cut into this body
to the fingers' limits
I decode my belly
I savour my breath
I navigate in my veins
with blood's speed

The breezes rest on my cheek bones
My hands touch things
Against my flesh your flesh settles me

Often   by being my body
I have lived
And I am living

Often   from a point without place
I glimpse   this body
pounded on by days
assailed by time

Often   from a point without place
I stifle my story
From past to future
I conjugate the horizon

Often   from a point without place
This body   I distance it
And from this very stepping aside
alternately
I live.

Translated from the French by Harriet Zinnes

Malak'Abd al-Aziz

We Asked

We asked . . .
Keep the pearls in the shells
They should stay at the bottom of the sea, waiting
Hopefully one day the time will come
Pulling them from the depths of the sea floor
Casting them upon the shores.
A sunbeam will embrace them,
Penetrating warmly, lingering
In the heart of the oyster . . .

The light glistens
Pierces the silence and the secrets
The white pearls tremble
Under the sun, they quiver
And it shines on their faces
With the fuel of love, it emanates . . .

Let the pearls wait for the tide
Until it comes . . .
Waiting

And we ask
Let the pearls remain in the shells
Did you promise the waves would come?
And wouldn't overflow except on Our shores . . .
And didn't dispense to lands other than ours . . .
The only thing it longed for was to embrace our sand

Thirstily . . .
Dissolving into it . . .
Watering it . . .
Give and take?
We asked . . .

Translated from the Arabic by Pamela Vittorio

The Fall

When we entered the bazaars
We saw the veils of rose, of green . . .
And heard the prattle of the parrots,
Babbling every place.
The same empty words,
Smeared with oil and sweets
So that the artificial taste was concealed
and we proceeded with attentiveness.

At times, I had to dress for the circus, masked . . .
We'd stride above the tightrope – alone
And twist over the raised poles
We change colours like a banded chameleon
Which we overcame – and fell upon the truth
Like the sharpened edge of a sword
And we tumbled from above the tightrope,
From the highness of the top, the vertical height . . .

Our platform raises, grows higher, higher
Rises higher and rises above the tentpoles, it springs
And with the touch of a hand
We bared the veils – we unveiled the secret,
And we stood still in the nakedness of the birth of purity and
innocence . . .

We gleam, we radiate – beneath the sun
in the nakedness of truth.

Translated from the Arabic by Pamela Vittorio

Joyce Mansour

Embrace the Blade

Hot night of the ramparts
Walls of Heraklaia
The thankless fretwork of the serpent on the smooth back
of the amphora
A woman's shell abandoned on the beach
Hot she too and drab
I remember that shape at the end of the path
Armed with desire and yet unborn
What oil full wine or sacrilegious draught
Filled this belly not so long ago
With its scented weight
A wave of blood hollows my bed
Empty empty empty
As death

Auditory Hallucinations

I would sleep until the mottled jaguar dawn
Surrenders to the deep blue-blackness
Charred forever
Rip my pain on the spiny bush
Of your tawny desire
I would sleep
A thousand deserts between us
Sodom and Gomorrah matchless pleasures
Obscene imaginings
In the air the bracelet of my lips
Forms the O of an unspeakable measure
Then the guards hidden
Under my tongue

Will shatter the millstone and its widow's vibrations
The whining wind rises
Love flows
The round muzzle of the afternoon quivers under bridges
Big white poodles follow the footprints of the fog
Capricorn
Your canines promise horror
The earth is shimmering with December
The rash bird buried
Let's repeat the song of the rain

The Sun is in Capricorn

Three days of rest
Why not the grave
I suffocate without your mouth
Waiting drains the stillborn sunrise
And the long hours on the stairway
Smell of gas
Flat on my face I wait for tomorrow
I see your skin glisten
In the black breach of the night
The slow surge of moonlight
On the inner sea of my sex
Dust on dust
Hammer on mattress
Sun on leaden drum
Still smiling your hand beats indifference
Cruelly clothed bent towards emptiness
You say no and the smallest object a woman's body can shelter
Bows down
Artificial Nice
Synthetic perfume one hour on the coach
For what pale giraffes
Have I left Byzantium

Solitude stinks
A moonstone in an oval frame
Yet another stiff-jointed bout of insomnia
Once more a dagger throbs in rain
Diamonds and delirium tomorrow's desiderata
Sweat of taffeta beaches without shelter
Lunacy of my lost flesh

Translated from the French by Carol Cosman

Seated on her Bed . . .

Seated on her bed legs spread open
A bowl before her
Looking for food but seeing nothing
A woman with eyelids eaten by flies
Moaned
The flies came in through the window
Left by the door
Went into her bowl
Red eyes black flies
Eaten by a woman
Who saw nothing

Translated from the French by Willis Barnstone

Last Night I Saw your Corpse

Last night I saw your corpse
You were moist and naked in my arms
I saw your skull
I saw your bones tossed by the morning sea
On to white sand under a hesitant sun

Crabs fought for your flesh
Nothing was left of your bloated breasts
Yet that's how I preferred you
my flower

Translated from the French by Willis Barnstone

Of Sweet Rest

Quickly take a pen
Write
I will steal I will steal
The orbit of the savage moon
The meagre sobs of the waves
Arriving from the other shore
Waves wavelets bandelets & twaddle
Write
Roll between my arms
Like a pebble between sky and the bottom
Of a well
Sand is the shield of the blind
On the parchment of his night
Quickly take some paper
Write
Follow me through the flowerbeds
Trenches crutches thorns
Listen
To the confidences of the rose
Chewed diced anodine
Go ahead write on the back of a tidal wave
Carve your signs
A thousand times enrolled
The mute joy of garbage
Submissive under the veils
Of the aquamarine

Trace
The indelible line
My green heart is smitten o spells of the moon
Sign resolutely with your proud cock
On the helmet & the snail's sealed head-piece
Write sign cross out
I drown in the inkwell of the slightest word
Never

Translated from the French by Mary Beach

I Saw the Red Electric

I saw the red electric
Hairs of my cleft
Climb up toward
My throat of plucked bird
And I laughed
I saw humanity vomit
In the fickle basin of the church
And didn't understand my heart
I saw the camel put on its shirt
And leave without tears for Mecca
With a thousand and one
Sand sellers and
Dark crowds like scaly dragons
But I could not follow them
For sloth won out
Against my ardour
And daily habit resumed
Its disjointed toe-dance

Translated from the French by Albert Herzing

A Woman Kneeling in the Sorry Jelly

A woman kneeling in the sorry jelly
Of her menopause
Was knitting as she thought
Of lambs crucified
To the pleasures of the kitchen
And the long sordid years
Of the great famine
To come

Translated from the French by Albert Herzing

Desire as Light as a Shuttle

Why weep on the hairless skull of tedium
Odious or otherwise
Esthetic
Argumentative
French-style tedium
I know very well how to sew false eyelashes on to my eyelids
Agate expels hate in the pallor of a glance
I know how to imitate the shadow that closes doors
When love
Clicks its lips standing in the hall
Rereading your letters I think of our walks
The promises of summer lingering Place Dauphine
Yawn under cover
It is already five o'clock
Gone are the kites the docile paving stones the careless dust
Jumbled in the flower-bed squared like a kerchief
Bogged down the lewd glance
Wool piles up on the clothes rack
Night gurgles inert
A beautiful disorder on my table

Why weep over a bucket of blood
Why forage between the old man's thighs
Venice
I'm ready to cover you
With my woodland hollyhock tongue
Ready to chisel at my pelt
Steal from shopwomen
Jump the ditch with no skirts or blinkers
To sink still moist in your gimcrack arms
Why keep afloat make up have fun
Why answer
Why escape
The memory of your icy sleep
Follows me step by step
When can I see you
Without shedding tears
On me

Translated from the French by Mary Beach

Rachida Madani

Here I am Once More . . .

Here I am once more before the sea
smashing whole doors against the rocks
mingling in the same bitter rolling motion
sand and pearls
in the burning metallic waves
the jasmine of my childhood and the shriek-owl of hell.

Here I am once more before the sea, bent over
under the annual booty of rancour
of fatigue
and of cocks slaughtered throats cut to no avail
for the well-being of a turban
which for a long time now has been
no more than a heap of dust
smirking under a slab
while in the shade of a fig tree
women and candles burn
to do magic with the eye
bad luck
and the raven of despair.

For an amulet did I too
swap my gold tooth
and the henna on my hands
and unclasp my eyes,
did I too look at the moon
and drink bowls
of the liquid verb, still and black?
I also kept staring
at the boats and the storks which were leaving
but we women all waited
                    in vain

in tears
for our fathers, loved ones
sons and brothers.

But the city opens wide the jaws
of its prisons
swallows them with its tea
and then fans itself.
But the city pulls its knives
whittles us a body without limbs
a face without a voice
but the city bears its heart
as we do our walls,
but the city . . .
I hurt even down to my shadow cast
upon the other sidewalk
where my latest poems are strewn
in little crystals of opaque salts
like icy tears.
My head falls down on my chest
like a mortar shell
seen from close up, my heart is a lake.

Translated from the French by Eric Sellin

Amina Saïd

On the Tattered Edges . . .

on the tattered edges of my unravelling memory
heiress of time
the water and sand sing in my veins

before my eyes springs
abundance ringed round by the barest deserts
of your horizonless freedom your prison without bars

you rediscover a destiny
in the figurines born of hard night
many strange things indeed
to search through until a name comes to mind

the madman and his monster
as though they were dying furiously digging
their own graves in the depths of violent sleep

and in the sands of memory
only the tracks of two bodies
and no one notices
the cold enemy
returning calmly
to prowl with the stark morning

they are only whispers
I shall go out under the sun
to sing with the loudest voice

Translated from the French by Eric Sellin

The Bird is Mediation

the bird is mediation
by virtue of wing
and song

and that palpitation
which gives it life

and that language too
a quest in the clear
silence of the night

if it travel down a road
of fire
between earth sea and sky
is it not reborn
aloft
from its trail of ashes?

like a soul which awakes
to the unknown
it will come from the tattered
heart of a cloud
to alight on the tree of the world

Translated from the French by Eric Sellin

My Woman's Transparence

my woman's transparence
has the whole sea
as its mirror

my sea-spray is born
of the salt of its peaks

my voice plays echo
to its thunder
and to its murmurs

we   were
as one sea-swell
when   we strode
toward land

we   joined hands

Translated from the French by Eric Sellin

And We were Born

and we were born
without the slightest choice of worlds

the wind gathers
our solitudes
leaves branches trees
our bodies strangers to eternity

there is a land in us
which feeds our dreams
from within

just as the night
secretly
feeds the night

by an intuition of the world
we sensed the blind
shore
the unforeseeable place

what are we going to
begin anew?

Translated from the French by Eric Sellin

The Africa of the Statue

the africa of the statue
flows out in a sawdust
of blood

a split belly
a speckled cosmos
scarified spikes
aslant in the sun

griots discover
that they are the stuff of memory

they bump
in fragments
up against the sky and the shore

and hasten
to rebuild our legends
with their wounded words

the dream of the past
is as a future

Translated from the French by Eric Sellin

On the Fringe

on the fringe of nothingness
on arpeggios of light
we erect frail structures
mediations of dreams and silence
as a defiance of the agony of being

we are so vulnerable
that to dazzle us
only takes the word which is immediate
and infatuated with the world's echoes

to us the image is the root
and words are its sap

bewitched by the void
obsessed with form we know
the outer limits

we who admit to the ineffable
know it well
the shadow's share
forever untamed

harassed from the outset
subject to real time
we shall one day return anew
to be one with our own coherence

Translated from the French by Eric Sellin

The Vultures Grow Impatient

1

the vultures grow impatient
with this man between two worlds
counting in his language
the alphabet of passion
the origins of the wind
the long delights
the daylong solitudes
and the secret of others
the stars and their paths
the branchings of coral
and their metamorphoses
the words strung
on the thread of pain
the forgetting of what endures

the anointment of another life
in one's arms
he would seek an abode
in the dizziness of an echo
the presence in the midst of things
of a day as naked as a woman

her spine uncurled
in stormy sleep
the language inherent in bodies

2

in order that our real
place be a place created
we must isolate the vision
of a higher life
that time recede from us
from age to age
that infinity lose sight of us
that the heart the better to understand
become the prey of the world

Translated from the French by Eric Sellin

West Africa
Benin
Ghana
Nigeria
São Tomé e Príncipe
Senegal

Irène Assiba d'Almeida

Sister, You Cannot Think a Baby Out!

Day after day
Week after week
Month after month
Life within me
I, amazed to feel it grow
Unable to comprehend
the mystery
I, afraid of pain
Not like anything I know
Is knowledge power?
Is ignorance bliss?

The first kick, energetic,
Pleasant, moving pain.
Will the rest be the same?

An old Lamaze book
On a dusty shelf
Breathe in, breathe out,
Breathe life.

Sisters laughing at you
At Lamaze too
At all the books you read!
When pain tightly grips
And Queen Nature reigns powerful,
Who remembers?
Sister, you cannot think a baby out!

Giant octopus
Tentacles in disarray
My body knows not
How to channel the pain.

A lull at last
Soothing balm on a raw wound
Then, suddenly, a dam gives way
The water breaks.
Surprised at the mighty flow
I lie, soaked in pain and fear.

An iron hand grips my womb
And viciously lets go
grips, lets go,
Again and again
Faster and faster
Sweating pearls all over my brown skin
Eyes wide open in disbelief
Never knew I could be
such a good contortionist!

Exhausted
I muster my energies
Like a volcano
Erupting a living force!

A last pang, excruciating
And, before I know
A thunderlike scream goes   .
As comes into this world
The baby
With the joyous scream of life.

Yes, I know
You cannot think a baby out!

Ama Ata Aidoo

Gynae One

'Kwaakwaa'
'Yioo yie'
'Kwaakwaa'
'Yioo yie'
'Alatampuwa'
'Yenyim dzi'

Alatampuwa   Yenyim dzi

Trolley out,
Trolley in.
Trolley out,
Trolley in.

Getting scraped
lying in
'vestigating only.
Post-partum complications:
Tying it up
Throwing one out.
Removing it all.

Dying for it
Dying with it
Dying from it.

Or
just
dying
dying
dying
dying.

Only corner of the
only world
where
water
must surely be
thicker than
blood.

All agony,
no
ecstasy.

For,
he
comes and stands with
a sheepish grin that
tries to
hide the
scowl and
fails.

Often
he doesn't come at all:
'can't be bothered'.
Or
He's run to Lagos in
panic and naked dread?

There
she lies,
the lamb.

Rounded limbs:
dimpled cheeks:
dewy lips
parted
in farewell to a

barely
understood
life.

And they said
they didn't know
much about
anything:

except
that
there is a God
and

He is a man.

Issues

We met
them
daily in the
queues:
the mother and the children
for whom she'd got
the best recipes for
cooking
stones.

Walls do not stare like
a brother's eyes.
One day,
mother shall raise
her head
face falling with
marvel

at what
forever-pregnant time
can
sometimes
deliver:

a three-legged lamb
or
human child,
who will come
teething
straight out of the labour-ward
at six in the morning:
slit itself open down the middle,
embalm
his own crevices with
diamonds
between
seven,
                    and
eight,
                    and at
nine,
from across the street
above the roar of the traffic and
other latter-day wonders,
scream at you
His-Lady-Love:

'Please shut up
questioning
my
money's
source, and

just do
me
the favour of
spending
it.'

For Kinna II

But
He said:

Princess,
– and remember royalty
are
made
not
born –

it is not for lack of what
you
could
have
had.

Step up this way and see
these valleys of
green grass that
the winds
the rain and
forever-sun have
rooted so firmly,
fanned up and
levelled down
as though it was a
UN proto-farm.

All that
can,
should,
must be yours.
If I could
drive the malaria from my bones,
accept what I cannot accept,
                              then
lift
up
my
gun and . . .
shoot.

Here on either side of
the great precipice,
time has not begun to get
restless:

the winds are so still
I asked a toucan for a drink, and
he heard me!

Ah,
the land is truly beautiful.

The cattle are healthy,
their udders are full.
And they might even
smile – at milking.

Especially now that their
milk and their
meat go to
                        far away places to feed
mouths that are less
hungry than our own.

As happens to the potatoes
we till
so slowly
so painfully:
using
ancient implements,
hoeing and
brushing.

Baby,
it couldn't have been
you that I
feared.

The noises
the praises
the blame:
and
affection running as
thin as flax in the hands of a crippled dame,
and
my love
pawed by
rising expectations and
rocketing inflations,
just
couldn't
fare
better than a fat mouse
before a lean cat.

They say
they mean
us all to

        walk
        swim and
        fly?

What do we do, but
crawl into
corners and die
who were born without
>   legs
>   fins or
>   wings?

No,
there are choices I
couldn't face
even for
you,

My Little Queen.

Totems

I
came upon an owl
at the crossroads
blinking with confusion
greater than
mine!

Bird of doom.
Bird of promise.

Fluorescent lightning on a
city corn-field,
tell the owl of
the changing times.

They-of-the-Crow
cannot
carve out

destinies through
marriage.

Whoever can?

He does
too well by her,
                              and
she always
knows when
starched rags go to swaddle
another's baby.

Dodua of the light palms:
She is hanging out the
last new to dry from its
first washing.

Perch where you can, and
tell your story. They make
us believe that all roofs
cover homes from the rain.

Akua my sister,
No one chooses to stand
under a tree in a storm.

So
You
shall not be the one to remind
Me
to keen for the great ancestors and
call to mind the ruined hamlet
that was once
the Home of Kings.

Itu kwan
ma
Adze sa wo aa
na
Adze asa wo!!!

Abena P.A. Busia

Liberation

We are all mothers,
and we have that fire within us,
of powerful women
whose spirits are so angry
we can laugh beauty into life
and still make you taste
the salty tears of our knowledge –
For we are not tortured
anymore;
we have seen beyond your lies and disguises,
and *we* have mastered the language of words,
we have mastered speech.
And know
we have also seen ourselves raw
and naked piece by piece until our flesh lies flayed
with blood on our *own* hands.
What terrible thing can you do us
which we have not done to ourselves?
What can you tell us
which we didn't deceive ourselves with
a long time ago?
You cannot know how long we cried
until we laughed
over the broken pieces of our dreams.
Ignorance
shattered us into such fragments
we had to unearth ourselves piece by piece,
to recover with our own hands such unexpected relics
even we wondered
how we could hold such treasure.
Yes, we have conceived
to forge our mutilated hopes

into the substance of visions
beyond your imaginings
to declare the pain of our deliverance:
So do not even ask,
do not ask what it is we are labouring with *this* time;
Dreamers remember their dreams
when they are disturbed –
And you shall not escape
what we *will* make
of the broken pieces of our lives.

(1983)

Mawu of the Waters

With mountains as my footstool
   and stars in my curls
I reach down to reap the waters with my fingers
and look!, I cup lakes in my palms.
I fling oceans around me like a shawl
and am transformed
into a waterfall.
Springs flow through me
and spill rivers at my feet
as fresh streams surge to make seas.

(1986)

Gladys May Casely Hayford

Shadow of Darkness

Shadow of Darkness, listen I am calling.
Night comes upon me, heavy dew is falling.
You are powerful as the night!

Your breath is sweet as the earth.
Your eye more gentle than a woman's.
Your horn, the curved bows of two moons.

On your forehead is the star of morning,
On your back the eagle;
Under your tongue the hump of beetle,
Beautiful bull from the line of Osiris.

Your feet are beautiful in strength
Your voice is deep as the thunder.

Listen I am calling, calling, calling.
Oh, I need you; I am lonely.
Come to me quickly – Shadow of Darkness.

Rainy Season Love Song

Out of the tense awed darkness, my Frangepani comes;
Whilst the blades of Heaven flash round her, and the
    roll of thunder drums
My young heart leaps and dances, with exquisite joy
    and pain,
As storms within and storms without I meet my love in
    the rain.

'The rain is in love with you darling; it's kissing you
 everywhere,
Rain pattering over your small brown feet, rain in your
 curly hair;
Rain in the vale that your twin breasts make, as in
 delicate mounds they rise,
I hope there is rain in your heart, Frangepani, as rain
 half fills your eyes.'

Into my hands she cometh, and the lightning of my
 desire
Flashes and leaps about her, more subtle than Heaven's
 fire;
'The lightning's in love with you darling; it is loving
 you so much
That its warm electricity in you pulses wherever I may
 touch.
When I kiss your lips and your eyes, and your hands
 like twin flowers apart,
I know there is lightning, Frangepani, deep in the
 depths of your heart.'

The thunder rumbles about us, and I feel its triumphant
 note
As your warm arms steal around me; and I kiss your
 dusky throat;
'The thunder's in love with you darling. It hides its
 power in your breast.
And I feel it stealing o'er me as I lie in your arms at
 rest.
I sometimes wonder, beloved, when I drink from life's
 proffered bowl,
Whether there's thunder hidden in the innermost parts
 of your soul.'

Our of my arms she stealeth; and I am left alone with
the night,
Void of all sounds save peace, the first faint glimmer
of light.

Into the quiet, hushed stillness my Frangepani goes.
Is there peace within like the peace without? Only the
darkness knows.

Catherine Obianuju Acholonu

Going Home

I

Our hands grope in vain
the springs have dried up
leaving us with
salt water
and we remember
the days
when the hooting of the owl
sanctified our mortality

we stand paralyzed
like skeletons
mounted
on the sandy soil
struggling against
the dry wind
blowing sand into our eyes
which have since ceased to see

footprints of blessed ages past
deeply backed on to the soil
show the way to the horizon
and beyond
but we cannot reach it
you and I

our kisses bite
like grains of sand in the eye
then our bodies touch
like two scaly fish

we stand paralyzed
like two accursed.

II

We plunge ourselves
into the abyss
mindless of the outcome
our blind eyes
surveying the darkness
and in the labyrinths
we grope and sniff
for signs of our
brothers
in the catacombs
at the gate
we present our printed
tickets
decaying lips
toothless gums
cracking laughter

shameless folk
that seek entrance
into the land of their fathers
you cannot partake
of the communion
without your *ofo*
without your *chi*

and we are back
at the cross-roads
dreading once more
to cross the horizon
having shed our outer shell.

III

Contact telegraphic
our sons speak
a foreign language
devoid of feeling
devoid of meaning

what choice have we
but to take refuge
in *ogbanje*
passing excrement
into the mouths
of our daughters
our ever mourning mothers

home again and yet
homeless
a dreary failure
for a nameless folk.

The Spring's Last Drop

I can still recall their laughter
As they spoke of 'lost virtue'.
I, Obianuju*
I have learned to live in scarcity.

So, cautiously,
i choose my steps
labouring up the steep hill
bearing on my head

*Obianuju: an Igbo name meaning 'one who comes in the midst of plenty and abundance'

in a clay pot
the spring's very last drop

but from the bushes
a sweet melody
streams forth
and fills my ears
disarming
tantalising

and the body
is tempted to sway
leading the feet
off the straight path

and the eyes
are tempted to stray
to find the source
the giver of temporal joy

but i must hold fast
my pot of spring water

Though the seller of clay pot
    never makes the 'customer'
though the carrier of clay pot
    be the mother of an only son
and though this tune
    vibrating in my ears
    tempts me to dance
    to sway my hips
    in unison
    with it
    beguiling

yet i cannot lose it

this stem
this prop

i have laboured up this hill
through toil and sweat
and i cannot spill it
this water so pure
so clear and sweet
the dying spring's last drop

i obianuju
i shall provide my children
with plenty
i shall multiply this drop
they will never taste
of the wasted fluid
of the sea

The Dissidents

. . . and the daughter of my father
she spoke to them again
from the top of the hill
from the heights of the land
from the storm raging
she lifted her arm
and like lightning
she quelled the storm

. . . and the daughter of my father
she shouted at the heavens
forcing the sky to release the rains
and the rain came in torrents
showering hot pebbles
on their bare skins

. . . and the daughter of my father
she said to them
wash!
she gave out white chalk
and they painted their toes
she gave out kola nuts
and together they ate
to appease the angry earth

and amadioha* spoke
through lightning and thunder
striking his death-mark
across the sky
yet they stood their ground

the rain struck harder
on their faces
and from the hills
the waters stormed
down the valley
washing the earth
and licking their feet
with feverish tongues
then the younger ones
rushed from the spot

and the daughter of my father
she raised an arm to stop them
but in that instant
amadioha struck
lashing black fire
on the dissidents
earth sucked their blood
and all was still

*Amadioha: Igbo god of thunder

Harvest of War

something is taking its course
   wailing echoes
   and re-echoes
   through long corridors
   of life and death
   where four roads meet
   where two roads cross
   where four roads meet
   there is coming
   and there is going

   allow me to use
   your oval passage
   o maid
   after the hospitality
   after a sojourn
   of nine moons

   may I wriggle
   through
   the bush-path

   there are streams
   of blood yet to be spilt

I crossed the seven seas
and planted myself
a seed that grew
in water and blood

and now
to let me a lease of life
she lies
plucking pangs of pain

gliding on the chess-board
of life and death

forgotten is the ecstacy
the pineapple-sweet apple
mutually devoured

it's harvest time
the farm is all ablaze
and she
undaunted and fearless
searches the heart of the fire
for the seed
that planted itself
in water
and blood

it knows neither day nor night
neither war nor peace
no danger even in the face of death
a world in a world
a subtle settler

another harvest
and you wet the soil
with teardrops
bring a spade
bring a coffin

   there are no more coffins
   wrap it up wrap it up in a mat

Other Forms of Slaughter

there were other forms
of slaughter
you know

when hands of sandpaper
jar at tender tendons
of daughter drums

when rods of aggression
rip through sealed valves
of reed flutes

when innocent virgins
basking in the sun
suddenly wake up to
greedy eyes
lecherous tongues
and devouring breath

and gathering their clothes
about them, clamber
hurriedly
up the cliff

but heavy boots
are at their heels
heaving chests pin
them down
then greedy hands
rummaging

tear open
the frills of their
delicate legend

unfolding a lustful era
of anarchic bestiality

yeah!
there were other forms of slaughter

Water Woman

i

owner of the drink of life
a cupful in my palm
and I gulp
to quench this fire
this dryness in my throat

beauty that blinds the eye
that breeds the insatiable thirst
in a man's bosom
slimy
tender
source of all woman's vice
fire that burns in water

you have your wish
o water woman
your wish is law
daughter of the river
you goddess of the silent sea

who am I to disobey
what am I to complain
our mother calls
mother snake chooses
her little one

for a meal
or to break her firewood
at the sea's bottom

ii

the reeds are waving at me
swaying this way and that
singing the song of the beautiful
the song of the rich
and I must hurry and follow

the lotus flower smiling
smiling on to my face
beckoning and reassuring
drawing my heavy feet
along the soft white sand
then the tide rises
and the waves throw up
their watery tongues
to welcome my shaky limbs

one moment
and the water meets my feet
pouring the peace of a lifetime
into my hungry being

and I must hurry and follow

iii

my sealed lips break open
and I hear as from miles away
the song of the water woman
now the rumbling of thunder
causes the waters to open

and my eyes fix
on that blinding beauty
darkness fills with the image
of the spectral majesty
sitting on a throne of snakes
the sacred python
round her uplifted arms
she beckons with a steady nod
and I plunge
making for the riverbed

discarded lifeless figures
skeletons
hooked on to mangrove roots
make little impact
and I try in vain to reason . . .

    when death comes
    the dog will not smell even shit

Ifi Amadiume

Nok Lady in Terracotta

If I were to write with my blood,
dip deep in the stream of my tears
to tell what sorrow my heart bears,
still I would not have made history,
as I seem not the first to tell my story;

Sad-eyed Nok lady
captured here in this terracotta,
I see reflections in your valley;
that fine deep curve
moulded by the course of sweat-drops
which have run down your brows,
mingled with your tears,
trailing down to leave
the telling marks of time
at the corners of your eyes,
running to the very base of your cheekbones;
delicate, mysterious to the stranger
but special truly to you
Nok lady.

And sad-eyed sisters I see daily,
I know by your looks,
though recorded in no books,
we too have travelled the same road,
carried the same load,
and sipped of the same sorrow;
knowing we are the beginning of
that distant road of long ago –
the very basis; the grass roots –
the mystery and secret of which
locks behind those sad lines

running along the curves
of the eyes of the Nok lady in terracotta.

Sister-tears of denial I share today;
same sap which ran through the mother stem
now runs in her off-shoots and grows on;
once ploughed, she will crop,
though she reaps not what she sows,
for the planters pick her harvest;
pitcher of water, not your water;
river-bed carrying not your water;
so mother do you carry their sons
who in turn will marry off your daughters!

Weak-kneed sisters sitting trembling
with nostrils flaring
and that rhythmic shake of the feet,
telling tales of anger and defeat!
Weep not sister, you are not alone,
for you are just one branch of the tree –
The Tree of Life; The Tree of Africa;
stretched out across the black land
is that dark mysterious valley
between the legs of Great Mother Nile,
the cradles of our birth
we dare not deny.

Still Mother!
you should not have flirted,
mating with the current
to give birth to civilization,
deserting your children
in your careless amorous trips
between the current and the sun.
Your sons in vengeance,
did they not desert you?
appropriate your daughters?

take control of the lands?
seek alliances exchanging sisters?

Mother!
you were thus left neglected,
those sons left you unprotected,
then the rape began:
persecuting Persians!
merciless Macedonians!
ruling Romans!
ruthless Arabs!
torturing Turks!
treacherous French!
leech-like English!
You see sister,
the beginning of our anguish.

They too cunningly control lands,
mindlessly exchange sisters,
purposely pass on knowledge
controlling your minds
as you deny yourselves
and refuse to look into her eyes –
the eyes of the Nok lady in terracotta.

The Union

1

You stay far far away
and unreachable to me.

Although my soul,
like a baby,
seeks nourishment

in pure flowing nectar
from its mother's bosom,
you go far far away
so unreachable to me.

You stay far far away
leaving a lead
weighing heavily
on my gentle soul
which seeks
only to see you.

2

Tonight,
my love,
as I burn in loving,
I could turn a rat,
cut tunnels,
walk on all fours,
just to reach you.

As I burn in loving,
I could grow wings,
cross the sky,
to reach you.

As I burn like cinder,
I could dissolve
into thin air
just to reach you.

You remain far away,
maddeningly near,
Yet far far away,
so unreachable to me.

3

Ah one loving embrace,
to end a journey
well begun.
Do not deny,
my love,
this closeness.

To send,
in welcome,
a carpet of colours;
rainbowed spirals;
a path
studded in diamonds;
stones so precious;
a hand full of stars;
and you
at the other end
of brilliantly
lighted ringlets
beckoning on me.

In ripples of laughter,
glided half-way to you,
before I woke up
like one
gay in ecstasy.

You see,
I know you
even in sleep;
I know you
when you tease;
I know your shadow,
I know your scents,
I know your essence;

Sweet beloved
for that embrace;
the final becoming,
I complete the journey.
Take me now.

4

Awake,
asleep,
you come to me
fleetingly
like a sweet breeze
I cannot catch
in the palm of my hand.

Awake,
asleep,
I see you
sweet,
serenely haloed
in purity
I cannot hold
in the gaze of my eyes.

Awake,
asleep,
you play on my mind
in such sweet
and gentle tunes,
tingles in my soul
that I cannot caress
with my mortal fingers.

Sweet beloved,
how long now
the final becoming;

when will my soul
cease to hunger.

5

My love,
my love,
today is unbearable
as my soul
pants in anticipation.

The pain is unsettling
as my heart misses a beat,
thinking its beloved
has come.

Ah for
a gentle touch of wind,
a tiny drop of dew,
one whiff of your scent;

just enough,
my love,
to keep my soul awake
as I await
that final becoming.

6

(why the veil?)
Do not shroud me
in silk cotton
and shimmery finery;
they,
like my bare flesh,
are of this

transient world –
only fit for worms
from which they were spun.

Leave me open
as I am,
for I do not know
where,
which point of me
the eyes of
my beloved
will rest on

Leave me
as pure as I came
for the final reunion
with my love.

7

How the eyes of loving
soothe me,
make my flesh burn
with desire
and my blood
jet swift,
clear as a fountain.

Feed, feed,
hungry soul
in the eyes of loving;

tonight, tonight,
the meeting,
the union.

8

Ah!
to turn the night
into grey,
denying me
the midnight sun!

You sat me
on a moving,
high,
fast,
flying plane
to a faraway place
my fear
refused me to reach.

How in the moment
of danger,
I sought my beloved.
I could not make
the holy sign,
not belonging
to that order;

I only sought you,
called out,
dared pronounce
your sweet name,
my love.

Perhaps tonight,
there will be more courage
to journey
with those unknown
to the brightness

glimpsed
in last night's sleep,
if only to sight you
sweet sweet beloved
light of my soul.

9

Why the generosity
of heart tonight,
the holding,
the squeezing
of hands,
as we burn
in longing
with words unspoken,
eyes luminous,
hands moist,
pain in our hearts.

Still I asked
only for the garment
next to your skin
to wrap me
till the morning dawn;
a gentle sleep
inside a red rose,
scenting you,
dearest my heart.

10

Secret, secret,
my love!
last night
in sleep,
sweetheart,
I saw

your own beloved
at rest in his tomb.

Ah what curiosity
made me open
the sacred abode.

What compelled
the quickness
of forehead
kissing the holy ground
in supplication.

What jealousy
left your own beloved
a miniature figurine
in a basket,
lid
hurriedly closed
in the quick exit
of an unworthy intruder!

O the blindness of love
that would have
none other
except you,
the joy of my heart.

Mercy,
my love,
in tonight's serenade,
let me hear just you,
let me see just you,
let it be just you,
at last,
for the nodal night
of bride and groom.

Mistress of My Own Being

Untied of all binding knots –
the tears and ties of time,
freed of haunting memories and regrets,
feelings of contentment rush on
like soft tidal waves,
till slowly, they envelop me.

Thinking of nothing,
wrapped up in my own warmth,
in scents and steam-blankets,
protected in my contentment,
I lie calm and supreme.

In this sweet sanctuary,
I have no need of food or man,
I feel no need for tomorrows,
no need for sound or voices,
only the soothing silence of the night.

Through the dancing folds
of the lacy petticoat of the window,
I see the yellowness of the night;
a huge brilliant eye in heaven
probing me.

In amorous splendour,
she throws out hands full of golden arrows
reaching for the hidden apples
in the folds of my mind.

Not even the sensuality of the moon
can move me now in my calm
Peace and contentment,
let those be my virtue,
as I lie calm and supreme,
Mistress of my own being.

Bloody Masculinity

Shall I be child of the full moon,
a slave to love
in seasoned womanhood?

Shall I dare worship yet again
starry-eyed in the temple of love
with maidens yet unbroken?

Shall I shed tears of blood
again in loving
while virgins bleed freely,
new initiates in love?

Will the source of my spring
again recede
at the blast of the unbending penis?

Will my womb at the sight of hotness
grow cold and shrink in the face of
bloody masculinity
in this peak of womanhood?

Bitter

If you were to squeeze me and wash,
squeeze me and wash,
squeeze me and wash,
and I foam,
again and again,
like bitter-leaf
left out too long to wither,
you would not squeeze
the bitterness out of me.

We Have Even Lost our Tongues!

Look,
O heartless ones,
look at our dying people.

There was a time
when for pennies
we filled our bellies;
akara balls,
moimoi,
rolling smoothly
from leaves
fresh and boiled;
beans,
steaming hot,
cooked in spice
and red oil,
fermented maize,
millet,
for porridge.
We broke the night's fast
for pennies!

Look,
O heartless ones,
look at our dying people
today.

The freed wife,
the old woman,
our mothers,
no longer find
grains, seeds, tuber
to cook,
to sell.

No more
the delightful
first morning sight
of schooling children,
running helter skelter,
steaming food bowls,
or black slates
in their hands.

Uniforms still fill the streets,
faces harsh,
eyes restless,
they are armed soldiers,
on the beat,
hungry for anything.

Look,
O heartless rulers,
look at our wretched people
today.

We went to the polls,
we won no respect,
we were losing, losing,
losing everything,
but our mouths.
We could curse them,
we could curse the land,
we could curse the day
they found oil in her.

As we grew
more desperate
with hunger and thirst,
embroideries,
fancies
on their shiny brocades,
shimmery silk gowns
grew more elaborate
and bold,
so too
tales of more oil
they sold.

Like mighty dreaded masquerades,
they claimed the streets,
indeed
every decent space
to themselves,
while our people
became glum,
tight lipped
distant spectators
waiting, waiting and waiting.

The soldiers have come,
still we have nothing,
nothing, nothing.

Now we have even
lost our tongues,
cut off
by the sharp edges
of khakis
stiffened with the juice
of our grains,
our tubers.

Look,
O heartless dictators,
people are dying, dying,
dying of hunger,
dying of thirst!

Creation

Like a sweet orange sucked by a boy,
you have sucked all the goodness out of me.
Still like a boy,
you did not know when to stop.

Like the seed of an orange spat out by a boy,
you have left all the goodness still in me,
still like a boy,
you have left my seed to crop.

I was left naked and unshielded by a boy.
It was not the nakedness of the naked;
it was the nakedness of the naked earth;
it was the nakedness of birth;
it was the nakedness of creation.

My seed took root again,
my shield in time regained,

full of sweet juice
again to be sucked.

Be Brothers

This garment I give you,
let it shield your body,
in return, please shield my baby.

Just as this garment hides your nakedness,
please hide his nakedness and weakness.

This garment I give you,
sewn with tender care,
in return, please take care of my baby.

Just as each stitch is sewn with tenderness,
please soothe his sadness and tender tears.

This garment I give you,
one for him, one for you,
in return, please be brothers with my baby.

He comes to you sad,
let him come to be glad,
all for this garment I give you.

Rashidah Ismaili

Bajji

Kinshasa, Lubumbasha
land of my male pride/
sower of my cubs
where is your lioness
whose carcass protects
your sun-scorched shoulders
whose need to breed your
pack is equal to the furore
of gunshots and knives
bloodshed and rugged crosses
born on backs of brave men
and sorrowing women
whose bosoms are uncovered
and left crying.

Cats forsaken are still
at one time kittens
and while you, O Mighty Kongo
run your course do you carry
the names in secret of those
who perished before Leopold's
finger pointing death to sons
and heirs of kings and queens
of Lualaba.

Lingala speaking ladies
with your lappas tied tight.
Your big buttocks fight against
the print you imprint the
outline of your bottoms
that move to the rhythms of
a lonely guitar playing

in an empty night.
Hands sore, feet tired
song strummed in a sorrowing night
  PATRICE IS DEAD!
I hear you, O Mighty Kongo cry
'My son is dead! Where is the one
Just one out of many who can bear
the weight who can kiss the sacred
grounds of my forests?'

I hear you, spacious plains/ green
and lush, crying in the wind.
I feel your tears in the dew stained
out between my toes; I cry.

Do you cry too, o traitors vile
and villainous fools? Not brothers.

Do your acts make you Cain/ Abel
reincarnate that your burdened heart
does not bleed before the loving gaze
of the SON OF AFRICA. Bleeding
bending over in pain. Glasses crushed
against his face like his dreams for you
seen but not realized/ broken but dreamt
just the same.

Can you sleep now in palatial security
beneath the shadow of your deeds
in the comfort of foreign arms cache
to buy your safe dreams while miles
and miles away in the forest of new
lands your empty house stands waiting like
death's door opening?

Solange

You are pretty Solange
  Your skin is fair.
  Your waist so slim.
You are lovely.

You are beautiful Solange
  long legs
  long arms
fingers with an octave span.

The colouring around
  the rim of your fingers
  the tinge of your ear tips.
But . . . your eyes are green
  even though
your nose is wide
  your lips full,
your backside round and high
  Your feet slightly flat:

But your teeth are white as snow.
  And somehow/ all combined
you are a lovely mélange.

Solange you are tied to your father
  by the nose and
this cord that knots elastic
  stretching back to his mother
the one you look like.

Don't fret Solange.
  Don't cry.
I see your mother's print.
  Your eyes are Parisian dreams
and your hair has a mind of its own

like you.
Sometimes it would be French
Sometimes it would be Cassamance.
'Tis a pity Solange, 'tis a shame!
That the blood of just one man
could darken all your dreams
and discolour all your limbs.

Solange, you speak so well;
   so careful and sure
modulated concealing the
   muted rhythms of
your heartbeat.

You stare at black and white faces
   and hold yourself apart
from your lips/ from your nose.
What is a face without those?

Chemicals care for your hair
   which otherwise will not
be held within the confinements
   of style.
What is a head without curls?

You strap the buttocks that
   will not flatten
inside a Chanel line.

You look at yourself in a mirror
   refusing what you see
extracting parts from the whole.
   Praying in the night
for change to come.

Your Godmother lives in a castle
  in the Black Forest
with an ogre.
  She is a fairy. S/he masquerades.

But you are their reality.
  A little bit of this and
a little bit of that.
  But all in all Solange
You are quite beautiful.

Lagos

Lagos you are dirty
Your sand is soiled
Your fruits pithy.

I am tied to you
in a strange land
by lines that queue up
for foodstuffs you
should be eating but
ship off to me here
where I stand on check
out lines and marvel
at the cost of one
paw paw, just one mango
singular, along and apart
from you my dirty city.

O Lagos, your streets
are packed and pollute
the air while here in
a smug smogged city
I choke.

Your cord cuts my throat.
I am hurt and I cry like
my Mami market mothers
who go home night after
night with the same tin pots.
Their food is rotting and
ought to be thrown out to
the birds and beasts of
the forest/ but the lines!
O God, these lines are so long
and between the houses and
the foodstuffs so many palms
must be oiled.

Nairas are dripping with black gold
and yet a beggar man's lot is the
same/ He covers his shame as best
he can and little boys skip school.
A policeman holds his right hand out
a green car passes him dash. And we go
dash you dis and we go dash you dat
and mek we do business.

O Lagos, Lagos, ah say, you don tyah
fo dis? Yousef wey you de com fom?
Me, I long for the cleanliness of
sand roads that breathe long in carefully
spaced intervals between cars running
wild like mustangs roaming the plains.
There are no drivers to speak of.
They have vanished over hills and
into gulleys.

The seeds have been planted. It is a
bitter harvest we reap. The deeds have
been done. What has been sown is the
flower of our calabashes on the eve of

harvest. If only the waters in the Marina
    If only the waves would whisper
louder the secrets of her beaches I would
know all/

My harbour is named after a queen whose
son's footprints are planted like a bad
seed on the headdress of my children.

Lagos, lay your plans carefully. There
is no way to stop the rise of bicycles
and lorries, hopeful bodies and empty
pots. You divert dash for food, care
for business. We are not an oasis in a
dying desert/ Have we not learnt, o
Lagos, the sound of seductive songs
and sights that blind us
between need and life there *must* be hope/

Queue

There are long lines that
snake around kiosks
where few and paltry items
are stocked and dispensed
by dispassionate vendors
with hands overstretched
for coins before packages
are handed.

Oniybo! You are pale and pink.
Your snout honks when you blow
the horn of your car that lets
out an over-ripened tomato
burnt in Africa's sun.

You are tattooed by its foreign
touch. You walk fast but do
not touch your feet upon the
ground where you walk over
bodies covered with flies
and slap your pounds upon
the dusty counters into greedy
palms of those whose souls
are prodded by the fear of
hunger they see around them.

'*Mami wey tin ah de see?*' a
small boy asks his mother who
casts her eyes to the ground.
Obonyi, she says softly
waiting for the dust to settle
for the distant roar of a car
that spews dirt from a dusty
engine bought years ago for a
one-way ticket to Liverpool
by an Irish lady who met and
married a man named Tunde
who later left her to live
with Bayo.
Oniybo, you have taken the last
of this week's sugar/ your stomach
is already fat you shouldn't eat
so much. *Oniybo!* You are dirty
like the smoke that spurts from
your car exhausted it is your car
like you, tired and spent. You have
carried too much weight too long.
Your car wears down like the maids
you put to bed with hernias and
boys whose manhood you have stolen
that you wear around your neck

beneath the coloured shirt you like
to wear so much.
There is a line that curves around
an empty kiosk.
'*Oniybo! Do you hear?*'
There are empty stalls and pots tonight.
In the night you listen to BBC for news
from Rhodesia. A car roars, a cat knocks
over a can/ you start and tremble.
What's wrong? It was not always so.
You used to sleep well/ one gin and tonic
after meals and you were off to bed.
But things have changed.

You sleep lightly, *Oniybo*/ taking large
breaths of air. You don't sleep soundly.
Your snoring is off key, Sah! Your humour
is dour and drab like your grey coat you
throw over your arms when you go out in
the dark dark night.

Yet Still

I have been encouraged to wait
                    outside the door
to wait in an empty room
                    to wait for a
turn of a knob
                    to wait
for a room to fill
                    to wait and
be patient.
                    I have been encouraged.
I have waited outside the door
                    without word or hope

outside with space for company
                    outside
I have waited.
Inside you have sat
                    sitting inside
behind a door
                    sitting inside
a big room
                    sitting inside
safe from me
                    outside
where I have waited
                    tired of waiting
your door opens slowly
                    I am waiting.

Molara Ogundipe-Leslie

Nigeria of the Seventies

Ensconced now in your heart, our mother
To see you more nearly
Treading your breast now wary
Let the flowers sproud under our feet

To change you, mother of driven children
Amidst the noise, the cacophony of delirium
Arms lunging swathe, drive to strangle
Disperse the jaundiced visions!

They stand around us now, who were the
Objects of dreams, wraiths of conceived visions
Splice the pith from the bark!
Who would unlace the dream from the thing?

Desperate the noise distracts interminable
Ceaseless as our pleasure's music, the sensual drone;
They fly in the face of the sun, your children
Few reach to find the core, the noise's silence.

Tendril Love of Africa

I see again and again in my eyes
the smile flit over your cheekbones
Reach like a tendril to caress your face
in those lean days that startled
do you rejoice
that life does not slaughter our dreams
our secret thoughts on its butcher bench of time
that we gather to ourselves

the scraps and bones our dismembered being
hoard to nurse them
that death may not out-stare us?

Yoruba Love

When they smile and they smile
and then begin to say
with pain on their brows
and songs in their voice:
'the nose is a cruel organ
and the heart without bone
for were the nose not cruel,
it would smell my love for you
and the heart if not boneless,
would feel my pain for you
and the throat, O, has no roots
or it would root to flower my love';
run for shelter, friend,
run for shelter.

Rain at Noon-time

for Julius Nyerere

a feastful sight
you see them now our people
this noon of leavening shadows
come sit round together to
dance the dance of children . . .

you say . . .

dance the dance of rippling waters
as now our history gathers
the foliage hold their palms to the skies
faces frowning look up to the skies
in our lands where laughter weeps unknowing

dance with us a dance of the future
they will not let us sit in peace
nor let our eyelids droop in earned rest
and the flood comes that must

they will not let the raindrops say
rain time is peace time
for the bursting forth of joys.

(1974)

Maria Manuela Margarido

You Who Occupy our Land

Do not lose sight
of the skipping children:
The black khaki garbed snake
struts before the hut door.
The breadfruit trees they cut down
to leave us hungry.
The roads they watch
for fleeing cacao.
Tragedy we already know:
the flaming hut
firing up the palm-thatched roof,
the smoke smell
mixing into the smell of
guando fruit and death.
We know ourselves,
sorters of tea from hampers
bark-strippers of the cashew trees.
But you, faintly off-colour
masks of men
barely empty ghosts of men
you who occupy our land?

Translated from the Portuguese by Allan Francovich

Socope

The long green grasses of my island
are now the oca shade
mist of life,
on the backs bent over the load

(copra, coffee or cocoa – all the same)
I hear steps in the calculated
socope rhythm,
the feet-roots-from-the-earth
while the chorus
insists with a lament
(lament or protest – all the same)
dragging itself continuously
until it explodes
in a strong longing for liberty.

Translated from the Portuguese by Julia Kirst

Landscape

Nightfall . . . grass on the back
of the gleaming black man
on his way to the yard.
Grey parrots
explode in the palm trees' comb
and cross each other in my childhood dream,
in the blue porcelain of oysters.
High dream, high
like the coconut tree along the ocean
with its golden and firm fruits
like obstructed stones
oscillating in a tornado's womb
ploughing the sky with its mad
plumes.
In the sky the severe anguish
of revolt passes by
with its claws its anxieties its certainties.
And an image of rustic lines
takes over the time and the word.

Translated from the Portuguese by Julia Kirst

Roça

The night wounded
by a sharp spear
of rage
bleeds in the woods.
Dawn also bleeds
in its own way:
the dawn bell
awakens the cleared yard.
The overseer begins
to assign tasks
for another day of work.

The morning still bleeds:
you cut the banana tree
with a silver axe;
hoe the bushes
with an axe of anger;
open the coconut
with an axe of hope;
cut bunches of andim
with an axe of certainty.

And at sunset you return
to the slave quarters;
the night sculpts its cold lips
on your skin.
And you dream about a future
of a free life,
that your action
will bring about.

Translated from the Portuguese by Julia Kirst

Alda do Espirito Santo

The Same Side of the Canoe

The words of our day
are simple words
clear as brook waters
spurting from rust-red slopes
in the clear morning of each day.

So it is I speak to you,
my brother contracted to the coffee plantation
my brother leaving your blood on the bridge
or sailing the sea, a part of yourself lost battling the shark
My sister, laundering, laundering
for bread to feed your sons,
my sister selling pits of fruit
to the nearest shop
for the mourning of your dead,
my adjusted sister
selling yourself for a life of greater ease,
in the end only suffering more . . .

It is for you, my brothers, companions of the road
my cry of hope
with you I feel I am dancing
on idle nights
on some plantations where people gather
together, brothers, in the harvest of cacao
together again on market day
where roasted breadfruit and chicken will bring money.
Together, impelling the canoe along the shore,
joining myself with you,
around the brimming bowl,
joining in the feast

flying through
the ten toasts.

Yet our age-old hands part
on the immense sands
of the São João beach,
because I know, my brother, blackened like you by life,
you think, brother of the canoe,
that we two, flesh of one flesh,
battered by hurricane tempests,
are not on the same side of the canoe.

It is suddenly dark.
There on the far side of the beach
on the Point of São Marçal
there are lights, many lights
in the dark palm-thatched sheds . . .
the sweet whistle thrills –
strange beckonings –
invitation to this ritual night . . .

Here, only the initiated
in the frenetic rhythm of the dance of propitiation
here, the brothers of the *Santu*
madly wrenching their hips
releasing wild cries,
words, gestures
in the madness of the age-old rite.
In this side of the canoe, I also am, my brother,
in your agonizing voice uttering prayers, oaths, and maledictions.

Yes, I am here, my brother,
in the endless wakes of the dead
where the people play
with the life of their sons,
I am here, yes, my brother,
in the same side of the canoe.

But we want something still more beautiful.
We want to join our millenary hands,
hands of the cranes on the docks,
hands of the plantations and beaches,
in a great league encompassing
the earth from pole to pole
for our children's dreams
so we may be all of us on the same side of the canoe.

Afternoon descends . . .
The canoe slips away, serene,
on course to the marvellous beach
where our arms join
and we sit side by side
together in the canoe of our beaches.

Translated from the Portuguese by Allan Francovich and Kathleen Weaver

Where are the Men Chased Away by that Mad Wind?

Drops of blood drip on the earth
and the men dying in the bush
and drops of blood keep dripping
on those who have been thrown into the sea.
Fernão Dias is for ever in the annals
of the Ilha Verde, red with the blood
of those fallen
on the immense sands of the wharf.
Ah! That wharf, that blood, those men,
and the chains and the blows,
they resound and resound again
and sink into the silence of the fallen lives,
the screams and the cries of pain
of men who are no longer men
under the fists of nameless executioners.

Zé Mulatto in the annals of the wharf
executing men
amidst the thump of falling bodies.
Ah! Zé Mulatto, Zé Mulatto
Your victims cry out for revenge.
And the sea, the sea of Fernão Dias
that has swallowed up those human lives
the sea is red with blood.

– Up we stand –
Our eyes turn to you.
Our lives buried
in the death camps
men of the 5th of February
men thrown into death's oven
begging for mercy
shouting for their lives to be spared,
dead from lack of air and water,
they all rise
from the mass grave
and standing in a court of justice
cry for revenge . . .
The bodies fallen in the bush
the roofs, the roofs of men
destroyed by the storms
of incendiary flames
the burnt lives
they now form an unusual court of justice
and cry for revenge.
And you the executioners
and you the torturers
sitting in the dock
– What have you done to my people?
– What have you got to say for yourselves?
– Where have my people gone?

And I, I answer,
above the silence of those voices raised
to obtain justice:
one after the other, all in a line . . .
for you, executioners,
pardon has no voice,
the hour of justice is about to strike
and the blood of all those lives
fallen in the bush of death
that innocent blood
soaking the earth
in a silent shiver
will impregnate this earth
that cries for justice.

This is the flame of mankind
singing its hope
of a world without chains
where freedom
will be the only motherland . . .

Translated from Mario de Andrade's French version by Jacques-Noël Gouat

Far from the Beach

Brown harbour of our land
come and kiss the wild little feet
of my thirsty beaches
and sing, my harbour
the bloated bellies
of my childhood
our eager dreams
of my small world
wasted upon these sands,
of the brown beach of Gamboa

moaning on the sands
of the beach of Gamboa.

Sing, my child,
your howling dream,
on the far away sands
of the brown beach.

Your palm roof
At the edge of the beach

Your deserted nest
on market days.

Your mother, little one,
in the struggle for life,
a fish basket on her head
for her daily work
with the baby on her walking back
and you, my dream, on the brown sands
in your shirt torn
in a common destiny,
the long wait, the swollen thighs
Mother walking under the weight of life
mother walking for the fish to sell
and you, paddling on the sea waters . . .
   – Ah! The falling evening's catch in my bay . . .
and my placid mother
   and all that fish to sell.

Translated from Mario de Andrade's French version by Jacques-Noël Gouat

Grandma Mariana

Grandma Mariana, washerwoman
for the whites in the Fazenda
One day she came from distant lands
with her piece of cloth round waist
and stayed.
Grandma Mariana stayed
washing, washing away, on the plantation
smoking her gourd pipe
outside the slave-quarters' door
remembering the journey from her sisal fields
on a sinister day
to the distant island
where the hard labour
erased the memory
of the bulls, the deaths,
away in the distant Cubal.

Grandma Mariana came
and sat outside the slave-quarters' door
and smoked her gourd pipe
washing, washing,
a wall of silence.

The years drained away
in the hot land.

– 'Grandma Mariana, Grandma Mariana
it is time to leave.
Go back to your vast lands
of endless plantations.'

– 'Where's the people's land?
Old woman comes, never returns . . .
I came from afar,
years and years spent in this yard . . .
Mad old woman does not have land anymore
I will stay here, silly boy.'

Grandma Mariana, smoking her gourd pipe
at the doorstep of your dark alley,
old little Grandma tell us
your inglorious story.
Live, vegetate
in the shade of the yard
you won't tell your story.

Grandma Mariana, my little Grandma,
smoking her gourd pipe
on the doorstep of the slave-quarters
you won't tell of your destiny . . .
Why did you cross the seas, old little grandma,
and remain here, all by yourself
smoking your gourd pipe?

Translated from the Portuguese by Julia Kirst

Annette M'Baye d'Erneville

Requiem

To Adrienne d'Erneville who did not return . . .

Your final bed was not adorned with roses
Your shroud was neither white silk nor maternal cloth
No perfumed water bathed your body
And your tresses were not arranged with a comb of gold.
You spoke your fear of the giant bird!
You believed the fork tongue and evil eye!
Who could have thought, seeing you so beautiful,
That you were dressing for Lady Death?
Embrace of the night? Kiss of the early morning?
The sand of the desert has cast your curves
And burned them to a powder.

(Paris, 1952)

Translated from the French by Brian Baer

Labane

Our lost virginities will never be regained.
Never more will we be chosen from princely
beds.
   The Royal Eagle, with his pearly beak
   Digs into the slain hearts
   Ruptures the life roots
   Abandons the remains
   To the rapacious of his court!
   The first drop of blood
   Refreshes him, intoxicates him.

Oh! How pure we would like to be reborn
And let the other at our smooth flanks
Make a gift of his hands!
Would we be worthy of that again!
Oh! Lord! Save us!

(Diourbel, 1963)

Translated from the French by Brian Baer

Kassacks

To Ousmane, my son

You are a man, tonight!
You are a man, my son!
  By your bruised flesh
  By your spilled blood
  By your cold glance
  By your immobile thigh.

And your mother remembers
  Her night of love
  Her torn entrails
  Her silent groans
  Her open loins
  The envious looks of her wicked rivals
  The greedy suction of your flower-shaped mouth
The miraculous amulet that
– With the help of Allah –
Has guided your steps to this happy day.

You are a man, tonight!
You are a man, my son!
  By the cutting blade

By your tried sex
By your suppressed fear
By the land of the Ancestors
Gawolo! . . . sing of this new man.
Young girls with upright breasts
Cry out his name to the wind.
Selbe N'Diaye, make this little man dance.

You are a man, my son.
You are a man tonight
They are all here:
   Those of your first moon
   Those you call fathers.
Look, look at them well;
They alone are the guardians of the earth
Of the earth that drank your blood.

(Kaolack, August 1958)

Translated from the French by Brian Baer

East Africa
Kenya
Malawi
Mauritius
Uganda

East Africa

Kenya

Malawi

Mauritius

Uganda

Marina Gashe

The Village

Kanyariri, Village of Toil,
Village of unending work.
Like a never dying spring,
Old women dark and bent
Trudge along with their hoes
To plots of weedy maize.
Young wives with donkeys
From cockcrow to setting of the sun
Go about their timeless duties,
Their scraggy figures like bows set in a row,
Plod up and down the rolling village farms
With loads on their backs
And babies tied to their bellies.
In the fields all day they toil
Stirring up the soil with hands and knives
Like chickens looking for worms.
Nothing here seems to sit still.
Even the village church is like a favourite well
Where the 'Revivalists' with their loudspeakers
Never cease calling people
To confess their sins and drink the Water of Life.
At dawn men ride away leaving the womenfolk
To fend for the bony goats and the crying children.

Marjorie Oludhe Macgoye

For Miriam

Children, why do you fear, why turn away?
Do you not know these knobbed, harsh hands are those
that turned and pulled your brothers from the womb?
These red eyes saw you first. These swollen feet
tramped to fetch water for your father's comfort.
This failing memory was quick to count
shillings to school him with, He'll tell you how.
It is still I.

Why do you doubt? Fingers are hard and stiff?
Hard, yes, to lift pots from the fire, to hoe
the heat-cracked furrow, husk the grain, split pods,
smack children hard, but shapely, straight, complete,
supple and moving. Laughter? When did they change?
I don't remember. True, the cup shakes, the needle
evades the thread. Joints crack. Yet I caress you.
It is still I.

Dress yourself child. See how I cover myself
carefully, unless now and then fever shakes me
and I forget the time and place. Yet truly
first cloth was a puzzle to me, we were ashamed
at new-fangled ways. We knew our modest duties,
walked blithely then, lithe, dutiful, expectant,
laughed at the stranger. You laugh and I laugh too.
It is still I.

We hid from vaccinators by the river –
laugh, you can see me doing that, typical me,
with a baby crying loudly among the reeds,
the medical people furious, road and market
growing till soon we could not hide. No fear now
so long as you keep your blood to yourself and pray
separate bed and bedding. Now they cannot unmake me.
It is still I.

We cried for sorrow, stood rebuked, so turned
away to Jesus, changed and were made anew.
The pipe is broken and the beads dispersed,
the children schooled, the scriptures learned by heart.
I know new obligations, faces, buryings,
yet self of self in saviour still the same,
still hard, lithe, laughing. He returns myself.
It is still I.

This baby-face is pale, but see the features
line by line echo mine. This one will go to
school, that one also, one dig, one live in town.
You do not need to tell me. Have I not grown,
mounted steep stairs, seen whirling pictures speak,
eaten politely, begging whatever tools
they left out from my place. Old, no-one's fool,
It is still I.

Africa of your ancestry has not changed,
Is age recognized? The tissues are the same,
the blood, guarded and grounded, feeds new life.
The artery-paths have hardened into highways,
tacit exchange crystallized into cash,
the morning sunward spit dried on our lips,
migration stilled, yet Mother Africa laughs,
It is still I.

Things that were open when we thought them good
are now discreetly covered, breasts by clothing,
blood-feud by boundary-mark, weapon by holster,
paternity by collusion. Things that were covered
those times we thought them bad now lie wide open,
unwanted babies, unpaid cattle, ways
of tying up the womb. Though witchcraft walks
It is still I.

Can you recall a time *Misawa* was
as strange as *Jambo*? Then we fed on pulse,
millet and milk, saw our dreams come alive.
Don't talk to me of change, even of freedom:
I have seen changes and I am content,
was saved, am free. If tongue and temper wander,
flesh stiffen and decay, why do you fear?
It is still I.

A Freedom Song

Atieno washes dishes,
Atieno plucks the chicken,
Atieno gets up early,
Beds her sacks down in the kitchen,
Atieno eight years old,
Atieno yo.

Since she is my sister's child
Atieno needs no pay,
While she works my wife can sit
Sewing every sunny day:
With her earnings I support
Atieno yo.

Atieno's sly and jealous,
Bad example to the kids
Since she minds them, like a schoolgirl
Wants their dresses, shoes and beads,
Atieno ten years old,
Atieno yo.

Now my wife has gone to study
Atieno is less free.
Don't I keep her, school my own ones,
Pay the party, union fee,
All for progress: aren't you grateful
Atieno yo?

Visitors need much attention,
All the more when I work night.
That girl spends too long at market,
Who will teach her what is right?
Atieno is rising fourteen,
Atieno yo.

Atieno's had a baby
So we know that she is bad.
Fifty fifty it may live
And repeat the life she had
Ending in post-partum bleeding,
Atieno yo.

Atieno's soon replaced.
Meat and sugar more than all
She ate in such a narrow life
Were lavished on her funeral.
Atieno's gone to glory,
Atieno yo.

Letter to a Friend

for Okot p'Bitek

Why should I be ashamed
not to be black, when you, who are so proud
empty your years thinking of Africa
and leave Lawino weeping?

Why should I be afraid
for my sons. Half-black? They are not half anything,
not putty-coloured flaccid in your hands,
but golden and red-blooded.

I know what fear is:
fear can be lived with! know about language!
half-hearing can be lived with. Colour blindness
does not disable one for living.

Why should I mind
being out of fashion, which being white is?
One baby dies in three, songs, homesteads die –
we cannot afford fashions, competing with death.

Why should I be ashamed
if children shout behind me and mothers stand by
giggling at swollen veins, stockings, or simply
at a foreigner on foot?

Is it my discourtesy
to come among them unsupported by
the clan staff and the escort of the marchmen?
I know my place and can recite the ancestors.

Why should I be ashamed
to live among my kin on even terms?
Am I a bride, silent, with downcast eyes,
different? Then what cattle will redeem me?

You have to be different,
demanding why you were born as you were, not grateful
to have survived. In Europe there are few
noses like mine left, even shaped by chance.

Changing continents in midstream
is likely to create a mild upheaval:
there is no need to lament loudly, like a woman
chasing a runaway sheep in a tight skirt.

Some of us, I admit,
have a little pocket Jesus, like a *jok*
under a stone to keep their bearings right
but this, my king-sized Lord, works differently.

He was not ashamed
for being noticed, brown, hook-nosed, acclaimed
for the wrong reasons, for the same ridiculed,
exposing us to scorn and certainty.

He made us tough,
White, tender-hearted, insensitive, able to
survive brass models of the Eiffel Tower
and the Eurovision Song Contest.

I am sorry for you,
because you are so schooled in beauty that
the chips of Ukambani torture you,
when all black living should be art.

There was a time
when every Nilotic house was decorated
with patterns between parallel lines. No lines
appear to be parallel in my house . . .

This convergence
offends my white relations, but it signifies
(Gerald will tell you) deep disturbance in
African concepts of time; no patterns now.

Africa is too big for me, content
to be a Luo woman bearing children
property of the father till the tide ends.
Waggling the *chieno*? Hush, forbidden, forgotten.

Why flap an empty girdle to hard-earned tunes?
Am I Yoruba, to cast huge shadows with a twisted cloth,
an Arab, skirted to the ankles, marking
the target area with cyclonic lines?

This is enough for me,
I act no part, learn no lines, improvise
from two lives that I have, listen, restrain
my foot from tapping, consume my own smoke.

You must select
gold from a continent, staggering under the weight
in a country where you do not know your friend's mother
or his investment.

If you would take it
easy, my brother, you would hear women weeping
not only for being black, see freedom seized
not only from being black, fear white drums beating.

There is exploring
and there is limiting, bearing forth and burying,
there is fear and there is being at home, and being
my sufficient self. Why should I be ashamed?

A Muffled Cry

For Chelagat Mutai

There was a time I might have cried
high on the ant-hill and been heard
but the ant-hill is ringed with buildings belonging to men.
I cannot cry my rights.

There was a time I might have taken counsel
on what was mine and his, what ripe for reaping,
but things made lie among things raised and planted:
I cannot take my share.

Mwana Kupona binti Msham

from *Poem to her Daughter*

Daughter, take this amulet
tie it with cord and caring
I'll make you a chain of coral and pearl
to glow on your neck. I'll dress you nobly.
A gold clasp too – fine, without flaw
to keep with you always.
When you bathe, sprinkle perfume, and weave your hair in braids
string jasmine for the counterpane.
Wear your clothes like a bride,
for your feet anklets, bracelets for your arms . . .
Don't forget rosewater,
don't forget henna for the palms of your hands . . .

Translated from the Swahili by J.W. Allen; adapted by Deirdre Lashgari

Micere Githae Mugo

Look How Rich we are Together

When you loved me
you not only nursed
and nourished me
to a fresh wholesomeness,
you taught me
how to laugh
even as tears scorched
my burning throat.

You gave me everything
a fortune
that gave birth
to our present
treasure bank
and in time taught me
to deposit
not to take all the time.

Look how rich we are
together now!

Hold here, feel
how my heart dances with sheer joy
listen to that new rhythm you have created
those thrilling, caressing blood currents
that flow through my whole being
bringing home a million messages
telling me how I truly belong.

(1972)

I Want You to Know

I want you to know
how carefully
I watered the tender shoots
you planted
in my little garden.

Flowers now adorn the ground
the fruits are ripe
Come
bring a strongly woven basket
and bring with you also
the finest palm wine
that your expert tapping
can brew
we must feast and wine
till the small hours
of our short days together

Joy and love
shall be our daily
harvest songs.

(1972)

Wife of the Husband

His snores
protect the sleeping hut
but the day's
load
and the morrow's
burden
weigh heavily over
the stooping mother as she

sweeps the hut
bolts the pen
tidies the hearth
buries the red charcoals
and finally seeks
her restless bed

His snores
welcome her to bed
four hours to sunrise
His snores rouse her from bed
six sharp
Arise
O, wife of the husband!

(1970)

Where are those Songs?

Where are those songs
my mother and yours
always sang
fitting rhythms
to the whole
vast span of life?

What was it again
they sang
   harvesting maize, threshing millet, storing the grain . . .

What did they sing
bathing us, rocking us to sleep . . .
and the one they sang
stirring the pot
(swallowed in parts by choking smoke)?

What was it
the woods echoed
as in long file
my mother and yours and all the women on our ridge
beat out the rhythms
   trudging gaily
   as they carried
   piles of wood
   through those forests
   miles from home

What song was it?

And the row of bending women
hoeing our fields
to what beat
did they
break the stubborn ground
as they weeded
our *shambas*?

What did they sing
at the ceremonies
   child-birth
   child-naming
   second birth
   initiation. . . ?
how did they trill the *ngemi*
what was
the warriors' song?
how did the wedding song go?
sing me
the funeral song.
What do you remember?

Sing
   I have forgotten
   my mother's song

my children
will never know.
This I remember:
Mother always said
  sing child sing
  make a song
  and sing
  beat out your own rhythms
  the rhythms of your life
  but make the song soulful
  and make life
  sing

Sing daughter sing
around you are
uncountable tunes
some sung
others unsung
sing them
to your rhythms
observe
listen
absorb
soak yourself
bathe
in the stream of life
  and then sing
  sing
  simple songs
  for the people
  for all to hear
  and learn
  and sing
  with you

(1972)

Stella P. Chipasula

Your Name is Gift

for Helen

This little light of mine
I'm gonna let it shine.

(Spiritual)

About the pain the folk
tales were silent.
Now the night claws my dream
in the dark cave where desire
fuses the thirst, the dizziness,
and the tenderness
that glows on my face.
In this round home of wisdom
you dance tirelessly till
I am breathless, aflame
with pain and remembered passion.
As my hand soothes my belly,
I mould and polish you
till you shine in my heart.
You are the answer to my prayer,
the white beach sand, a gift
from your father's island,
the promised white bead
that will grace my neck.

25 April 1989

I'm My Own Mother, Now

Mother, I am mothering you now;
Alone, I bear the burden of continuity.
Inside me, you are coiled
like a hard question without an answer.
On the far bank of the river
you sit silently, your mouth shut,
watching me struggle with this bundle
that grows like a giant seed, in me.
In your closed fist you hide
the riddles of the fruit or clay child
you told before you turned your back
and walked, fading, into the mist.
But, mother, I am mothering you now;
new generations pass through my blood,
and I bear you proudly on my back
where you are no longer a question.

Shakuntala Hawoldar

To Be a Woman

To be a woman,
a shadow without form,
extinguished by sunlight,
Wombing meaningless men
in the endless chain of need;
To be worn on rainy days,
like colourless old shoes
groping between pots and pans
eyes in steam,
Streaming more than onion-tears;
to be a woman,
characterless like bamboo stalks,
to be scissored to shape,
a hedge against odd weather
and when asleep to fly
untrammelled like a bird,
to exult in the open air,
tossing between oceans and clouds
dreaming of trees kissed by the sun,
while their gnarled roots sink into the earth;
then to return with the weighted womb,
like a boomerang –
to believe that shadows have existence.

The Woman

What you love in me
Is a woman
Who invites you to discover
The vast continent within her.

She has fevers too,
In her aloneness,
Isolated by her thoughts
She needs the groping fingers of gentleness
Which will let her be in quietness,
Will not ravage her tranquillity
By convulsive thirst of breasts,
But consciously grasping
That sexless core of need
For she is a mother who warms her insides
Beside you,
Carrier of wombs for men
Who ache in their lost hours
For her who is the sea
Without change, without end.

You

You are an extended branch of me
Root of me, leaf of me, flower of me,
So why do you ask for tokens when the
Tree itself is your shade?
You are my breathing, my thinking
My suffering.
So why do you sorrow alone?
You need not ask, for all has been given in a distant time
Knowing that meetings could only be
Thro' these twisting paths,
Now when you stand there
Shattered and lonely
You are not alone
For in your breathing, thinking, suffering
There is one who weeps with you,
Who knows the secret furrows of your soul,
Who needs no tokens,

Who knows you are an extended branch
An ever spreading root, a greening leaf
An opening flower
Of that self-same tree, burying its roots
In the soil of sharing, of caring.

Destruction

I do not know what has destroyed you,
Maybe it was too much of loving
Or too little
Both strangely have the same face – mine
When I look upon my hands
That have caressed you,
Untied corded muscles of pain
On cool sheets
Spreading my hair upon your limbs
To inflame them,
How would I know
That I could darken your eyes
And bring down the blinds
Upon your soul,
Hurt you by wordless thought
Scoop out warmth from your centre,
Leave dark regions of despair –
I do not know how I've destroyed you
Maybe it was too much of loving
Or too little.

You Have Touched my Skin

You have touched my skin
Without entering my pores.
Do you know the sores inside
Festering in the dark womb of my mind?
But you have been content
To know me as an image,
Sometimes as a caricature,
Scribbled in the corner of your newspaper
To make you laugh
You have known me
As your morning cup of tea
Without which your day could not have begun.
Or perhaps as a spoon to stir the
forgotten sugar at the bottom to sweetness.
Or just perhaps a pillow which you might use
If the nights of your past haunt you.
But the core of me, the hunger of me,
The thirst of me,
How would you have known?
For I have been losing
Myself in the smell of the kitchen steam
And the clatter of pans in the sink
Rising in the night to hush the child
While sleepless I watch for the first rays of light.

You Must Help Me Gather

You must help me gather
Broken glasses,
Cigarette stubs,
Dead orchids from the vase,
While the stars gently fall
From the cold night sky.

You remember, when you held my toes
Between your fingers
Feeling them like hands and cheeks,
You remember how I stirred
Questions in your eyes,
While my sleepy fingers brushed your hair,
Counting moles behind your ear,
Whispering answers that you knew;
Now help me sweep the dust
Beneath the board,
Hide the empty plates behind the door
And then black-out back to back
While the stars are gently swept
By the early morning light.

I am Not Just a Body for You

I am not just a body for you
You have travelled further
Into me, with me, beyond yourself to me,
You have crossed boundaries
That encase me, enclose you,
Opened doors to new worlds,
Beneath new suns which know no settings,
Now you can cross oceans,
You will not leave me
A void like the silent shell on the shore.
You will be here in the rain
In the sunlight, walking, talking,
Laughing to the roofless skies,
You will be here in the sea,
In the storm, thinking, suffering, loving,
Merging in the million drops
Which know no bodies
No boundaries beyond this mystic mutuality

Where I am, where you are;
Now you can go to other bodies
Beyond this shore
Love them, stir them,
Give them all of you and me
I can enchain them, encircle them,
Encompass them all
With your love and mine,
Desireless and free.

Beyond Poetry

This is far too rich for poetry
Far too heavy for tears;
What is that thread that binds
My wounds to yours,
Till, bleeding, I can scarce recognize
Your dark scars from mine?

You have come a long way
Through the corridors of my mind;
I have travelled too, long distances
In your hazy memory,
And when we meet behind the blur of tears
You know that our meeting
Was not the casual need of a passing hour;

In you I have met men
Carrying banners to the mountains
Dragging their feet upon the stones;
In you I have seen the victor
Smiling at visions of glory;
In you I have also seen the broken
Idol of clay;
You have been my enemy barricaded in

Your silence,
Battering me wordlessly, soundlessly,
While I crumple up before your indifference.

You have been my friend,
When I stood clawing the air
Looking for mental footholds
In the shifting precipices of my mind
And you lifted me gently,
From the deeps of my thoughts,
Smoothened the creases
Upon my brow,
And silenced the queries in my eyes,
And in that moment I believed once again
In illusions of understandings
Beneath mounds of mistrust and hurt.

It is Not Just

It is not just that I am looking
For sofa-comfort in your arms,
Or a temporary fire now that winter is here;
You have quarried me enough
To know the weak crumbling recesses;
When you probe into my pores
You fill my days with wild singing,
And I carry a soft pink sunset
Instead of breasts when you are near;
You need not label this love
And weigh it down with words!
But you must know that I reach you
When the Moka sun sets behind the purple ranges
And the endless quiet of the night
Descends the mountains into my home.

To my Little Girl

She was little,
She did not know the use of shoes;
I warned her of the brambles in the bush, in the briars,
She laughed trampling my words,
Briars, under naked feet;
She knows, I sighed
There are no shoes which she can wear for briars,
brambles,
For she has seen me bleed,
Seen me bruised,
With my feet clothed and covered.

I Have Gone into my Prison Cell

I have gone into my prison cell
You are my guard,
And freedom my chain
I know that you guard me well
Against myself;
I may just ask too much
Or think too little
To fit your pattern
Or I may just want to breathe
The cool night air
And watch if the stars are really blue at night;
And of course you know that
Nights are sombre things
Not for contemplation or for light
And it's better to discuss things abstruse by day
When the night's enchantment
Will not make me feel my chains
Or hear the clanging of doors.

Assumpta Acam-Oturu

Arise to the Day's Toil

Wake up Woman!
The Cock is crowing;
It's three a.m.
Wake up – it's time to weed the fields
in the distant hills.
Sleep no more;
Arise from the burdens of yesterday,
Forget the hours of toil
In that hot sun
That arose when you worked in the field
But set while you hurried to clear the weeds.
In the dark you return, as you left,
To those empty cooking pots.
Alas! the day is over
When the family enjoys the day's meal
But before you rest your feet
A voice calls: Woman get me hot water!
With that you know it's over
Until the cock crows
And the circle begins again:
Wake up woman!
Wake up woman!

An Agony . . . A Resurrection

The seven hills shudder in silence,
Agony, pain and anguish
As the heavy guns thunder
And incessantly rock these hills
Interrupting nothing, nothing

For it was a familiar sound
A living reality of this land
A sound that had redirected this country's course;
Once prosperous, once the pearl of Africa,
Once the pride of its people,
Now sundered by hatred, soured by grief,
Now longing for revenge on itself.

For twenty years, blood has written
This country's history
Yet from the gentle heart come the waters
Flowing in patience, pride
As forever transforms the deserts afar –
A water – the Nile that swallowed
The corpses time couldn't bury.

On the seven hills stood beauty
From it one could see what one wanted to see
Ignore what one didn't want to see
But it was there, right before one's eyes:
Anarchy, conflict, confusion, corruption, ideology,
Slogan, that only feed this land with corpses
The skulls of Luwero, the monuments of Luwero
Now only tell, and inscribe in blood.

Rich in patience and hope, this land has waited
Under the perennial sun in those twenty years
The dawns of those years were a prayer, a rise in hope.
As her ravaged arteries bled to waste
A voice from the stream could only yell: never, never again!
Was it too early, or was the voice
Now drowning into the gory sunset
A transition that may one day draw
From its unknown source, a resurrection, a new spirit?

Central Africa
Angola
Zambia

Alda Lara

Nights

Languid African nights
dissipated in moonlights. . . ,
faded in mysteries . . .
There are songs of tunguruluas in the air! . . .

*   *   *

Wild African nights,
the noisy frenzy of the batucadas,
makes the cashew leaves tremble . . .

*   *   *

Dark African nights. . . ,
peopled by ghosts and fears,
populated by wizards' stories
told by black nannies,
to the white boys . . .

And so the nights are sad,
wild, dark, languid,
but sad . . . like the cracked
and wrinkled faces of the old black nannies . . .
like the tired eyes of the farmers,
like the solitude of the wide, but empty hands.

It is because the white boys. . . ,
forgot the stories
the black nannies
told them as they rocked them to sleep
in the long African nights . . .

The white boys . . . forgot! . . .

Translated from the Portuguese by Julia Kirst

Maria Eugenia Lima

Shoeshine Boy

– A shoeshine, master?

The knee quick
worried
bent.

Masters of coming and going
daily ritualist
rolling ball
in good coconut sauce
   already hardened fingers
   handle
   polish
   tap
the authoritarian shoe.

Out of the cloth and the shoe
breaks a rhythm
   Panquepam
   Panquepampam
   Panquepam
   Panquepampam.

It is the batuque speaking.
Now exultant, then tragic,
it is the batuque speaking
the remote language
of the Angolan forest.

   Panquepampam
   Panquepampam

Magic whistle
vanishes
a distant message
of *sobado* tribes

    Panquepampam
    Panquepampam
    Pamquepampam

cloth and the
bent knee
hands that beat the drum
sounds that form
and are transformed

    word
    existence
    cry
    presence.
    in the esplanade
    imperative.
    protesting
    the batuque

Batuque without echo
inside the covered ears
in the empty eyes
in the still faces.

    Panquepampam
    Panquepampam
    Panquepampam
    Panquepampam
    Pam!

– Ready, master, done!
thousandfivehundred.

The busy voices return redolent
sensational in empty words
urgently searching for the lost time
as if nothing important
ever happened.

End of the road,
almost disappearing in the horizon,
Shoeshine boy tap-dances. And plucks
on the rustic greasy box
quissange harmonies
marimba tunes.

And chants a languid song
of grave sonances, roars.

The evening falls.
The sun is a blood clot
The night comes
in a halo of pure anguish.

Translated from the Portuguese by Julia Kirst

Marketwoman of Luanda

Eh! Oranges, sweet little oranges
my lady!

She come from afar, from Catete
where is *batuque* and *quitanda*
comes from afar her smile,
smile that intrudes
spontaneously into our eyes.

Comes from afar her smile
always fresh, always open.

And the quick and firm step
on the red earth
already warmed by the morning sun
reveals in each footstep
the graceful, fine walk
of an ignored queen.

She carries her *miçanga* necklaces
bright coloured clothes
and on her lips – pouring out the colour of ripe *pitanga* –
the promise of love
which is the reason for her living.

She carries *miçanga* necklaces
bright coloured clothes.

Eh! Oranges, sweet little oranges
my lady!

Singing cashew nut or mango
maboque, pineapple, papaya
high and low Luanda
the Muceque and Sambizanga
know her cry well.

And some poets say
that the magic colours
which adorn her marketstall
were spilled from the palettes
of exotic painters.

Seductively she walks down the road
just as the bright day breaks out
she announces with so much grace

as if the very dawn
is announced in her.

Eh! Oranges, sweet little oranges
my la . . . a . . . dy!

Translated from the Portuguese by Julia Kirst

Madalena

Madalena
black freckled mulatto
beautiful
skin like *gindungo* and cinnamon
grated coconut heart.

Madalena is young – 'Does not know the years.
Seems to be twenty, might be nineteen
perhaps even twenty-five!'
But in the dull eyes
in the dry breast
in the dragging pace
thousand tirednesses,
Madalena is 100 years old.

Madalena
mother of seven
four with the *quimbundo* fever
and another, always another
in the accustomed womb

– In the white hospital, what is to do, *sinhôra*?
What is to do if it is the *quimbundo* disease?
What will the white doctor do

if not even *quimbanda* can save them
And money for this medication?

The man comes back home
unemployed every time!
What is to do, *sinhôra*?
It is up to God.

Madalena
mother of seven
three buried
four promised to Calungamgambe;

Madalena
inexhaustible womb
completely renovated
after each hecatomb.

An inaccessible picture by a painter
who kept it to himself.
Forbidden poem by a poet
who told the stories of Madalena
in a way
that even 'jesus-christinha'
(with Bandeira's surprise)
felt uneasy.

Madalena
eternal single mother
who was never a prostitute
(and will never be)
is the only substitute
capable of redeeming her namesake
the Holy Maria Magdalena.

Translated from the Portuguese by Julia Kirst

Amélia Veiga

Angola

I was not born from your womb
but I loved you each Spring
with the exuberance of a seed . . .

I was not born from your womb
but in you I buried
my longings
and suffered the storm
of a flower transplanted
prematurely . . .

I was not born from your womb
but I drank your charm
in nights of transparent
poetry . . .

I was not born from your womb
but under your shadow
I fertilized new offsprings
and opened my arms
to a transcendent destiny . . .

Angola,
you will not be the land of my birth
but you are the land of my womb.

Translated from the Portuguese by Julia Kirst

Wind of Liberty

From the heart of the earth
a hallucinated wind erupts
sweeping up . . . up . . . up
the dry leaves of the world . . .

Wind which moans and howls deeply
and wounds like daggers
the hearts of people . . .

Horrible and cruel wind
which despises and twists
and makes war without quarters . . .

And now crawls lamenting
then grows in fury
and howls like a thunder,
but it is in every sense
the WIND OF LIBERTY
that the astonished poor world
aspires to retain in its hands . . .

Translated from the Portuguese by Julia Kirst

Gwendoline C. Konie

We are Equals

Brother, I will not howl challenges
from a lofty mountaintop
like a female Goliath drunk on anger;
But like a noble hen eagle,
snapping the chains that bind me,
I will spread my wings wide
and gracefully soar to the sky.
I will shower you with dazzling light
bursting from the ball of my mind,
from my body and my blazing intellect
and burn the scales that blind your eyes,
as you bask in my warmth below me,
that you may see me as a human, whole,
not a body to quench your appetites.
On earth once again, I will nurture you
with the ripe fruits of my brain.
Fixed by my eyeballs, your eyes will soften
and slowly melt with understanding
and flow into mine as mine flow into yours,
our shoulders touching, merging in parity.
Then you will know that you need me
as I need you to complete my circle of being.
Your last chain link will fall from me
while your selfless respect embraces me,
and in your heart I will plant
the rare gift of my love and loyalty.

In the Fist of your Hatred

Like a worm I writhe in your tight fist
As you try to smother my voice
And my mind with your brutal grip;
Fear stalks the house of my brain
As your pepper-red eyes shout blood.

Your grip strangles my tongue
Your fingers sprinkle seeds of fear in my mind
And it sprouts like a raging bush fire.
You have set up fear as my companion
And I cringe from your bloodshot eyes.

Secret alarm bells sear my brain
And leave me burning with a wild rage
For I will not let fear swallow
My breath, my dreams, and my hopes!
My hidden courage will saw off your fist.

Southern Africa
Mozambique
South Africa
Zimbabwe

Noémia de Sousa

Poem of a Distant Childhood

to Rui Guerra

When I was born in the large house by the sea
it was midday and the sun shone over the Indian Ocean.
Seagulls hovered, white, mad with the blue.
The boats of the Indian fishermen still hadn't returned
dragging their clogged-up nets.
On the bridge, the cries of the blacks from the boats
calling the women melted with heat
with bundles on their heads and snotty youngsters on their backs
– ringing with a distant air,
distant and hanging in the fog of silence.
And on the scalding steps
beggar Mufasini was sleeping, surrounded by flies.

When I was born . . .
– I know that the air was calm and restful (they told me)
and the sun shone on the sea
and in the middle of this calm I was thrown into the world
already with my stigma
and I cried and howled – without knowing why.

Ah, but for the outside world
my tears died in the fire of revolt.
And the sun has never shone on me as in the first days
of my existence,
although the shining and seaside scenery of my childhood
constantly calm like a swamp
had been what guided my adolescent steps
– also a stigma.

More, still more: all the different companions
of childhood.

My fishing companions
under the bridge
with hook from a pin and a line of string,
my ragged friends from wombs round like calabashes,
companions in games and running around
by the woods and beaches of Catembe,
all united in the marvellous discovery of a nest of tutas,
in putting together a baited trap,
in the hunt of gala-galas and kissing-flowers
in chasing Xitambelas under the hot summer sun . . .
– unforgettable figures of my tomboyish childhood
loose and happy
black boys and mulattos, whites and indians,
children of house servants and bakers,
of boatmen and carpenters
coming from the misery of Guachene
or from the wooden houses of the fishermen.
Spoiled boys from the Post,
cheeky boys of the fiscal guards at the police station
– all brothers in an adventure forever new,
scrumping from the cashew trees in the *machambas*,
or secret raids on the sweetest apples,
companions in the anxious feelings of mystery in the 'Island of
Lost Ships'
– where no shout was without echo.

Ah, my companions squatting in the marvellous wheel
and mouths gaping from the '*Karingana wa karingana*'
from the stories of the old man of the Maputo,
in the black and terrible twilights of the storm
(the wind howling in the zinc roof,
the threatening sea battering the wooden steps of the veranda
the casuarina groaning, groaning,
oh inconsolable groaning,

waking strange, inexplicable fears
in our souls full of toothless *xitucumulucumbas*
and King Massingas turned into pythons . . .)
Ah, my companions sowed in me this dissatisfaction
day by day more dissatisfied.
They filled up my childhood with sun which shone
on the day I was born.
With their unexpected, luminous comradeship,
their radiant happiness,
their explosive enthusiasm
to make parrots with paper wings
in the technicolour-blue sky,
their wide-open loyalty always ready,
– they filled up my tomboyish childhood
with happiness and unforgettable adventure.

If today the sun doesn't shine like the day
in which I was born, in the large house
beside the Indian Ocean,
I don't let myself sleep in darkness.
My companions are my steadfast guides
on my way through life.
They proved to me that 'brotherhood' is not merely a pretty word
written in black in the dictionary in the bookcase:
they taught me that 'brotherhood' is a beautiful sensation, and
possible
even when the skins and the surrounding landscape
are so different.

So I BELIEVE that one day
the sun will come back to shine calmly on the Indian Ocean.
Seagulls will hover, white, mad with the blue,
and the fishermen will return singing,
navigating over the tenuous evening.
And this poison of the moon which injected pain into my veins
in nights of drum and batuque
will stop forever from disquieting me.

One day,
the sun will flood life.
And it will be like a new childhood shining for all . . .

Translated from the Portuguese by Allan Francovich and Kathleen Weaver

Call

Who then has strangled the weary voice
of my sister from the bush?
Suddenly her call to action
has vanished into the flux of days and nights.
She no longer comes every morning
exhausted by her long walk
kilometres and kilometres swallowed
into the eternal shout of *Macala!*

No, she no longer comes, wet from the drizzle
loaded with children and resignation . . .
One child on her back, another in her belly
– ever and ever again!
And her face which is summed up in her serene look
a look I cannot recall without
my skin and my blood opening up, shivering,
sensing discoveries and affinities . . .
– But who has forbidden her boundless look
to come and feed my hunger for sisterhood
that my poor table is unable to satisfy?

Io mamane, who then has shot the heroic voice
of my sister from the bush?
Which unknown and cruel horse-whip
has flogged her to death?

– In my small garden the seringa is in bloom.
But there is a bad omen in its purple flowers
in its strong barbaric scent;
and the cloth of tenderness the sun has spread
over the light mat of petals
has been waiting since summer for my sister's son
to come and lie on it . . .
In vain, in vain
and the chirico bird sings, sings on the garden reed,
for the child of my far-away sister
victim of the misty mornings of the bush.

Ah, I know it, that last time
there was a flash of farewell
in her gentle eyes
and her voice was almost a hoarse whisper,
desperate and tragic . . .
O Africa, land of my birth, tell me:
What has become of my sister from the bush,
who no longer comes to town
with her eternal children
(one on her back, another in her belly)
with her eternal charcoal-seller's shout?
O Africa, land of my birth
at least do not abandon my heroic sister,
you must sustain her in the glorious monument of your arms!

Translated from Mario de Andrade's French version by Jacques-Noël Gouat

Our Voice

Our voice has risen, conscious and barbarous
Over the white selfishness of men
Over the criminal cold of all
Our voice streaming with the dew of the bush.

Our ardent voice, sun of *Malangas*
our drum-beat voice that calls
our voice spear of Maguiguana
our voice, brother
has awakened, cyclone of knowledge.

It lights up remorse with its hyena-yellow eyes
and burns glimmers of hope
in the dark souls of desperate people
our voice, brother
our voice, a drum-beat that calls.

Our moon-filled voice in the night of despair
our voice beacon in stormy nights
our voice that files through the centuries old bars
our voice, brother, our voice of thousands
our voice of millions of voices that raise the alarm!

Our voice fat with misery
our voice that breaks chains
our voice of Africa.
Our black voice that shouts, shouts, shouts!

Our voice that has discovered
in the toad pit
the sorrow as huge as the world
of that simple word: Slavery.

Our voice ceaselessly shouting
Our voice opening up new ways
Our voice *shipalapala*
Our drum-beat voice that calls
Our voice, brother

Our voice of millions of voices
                    that shout
                    shout
                    and shout!

Translated from Mario de Andrade's French version by Jacques-Noël Gouat

Let my People Go

Warm night of Mozambique
and the distant sounds of a xylophone reach me
– distant and regular –
where are they coming from? Even I do not know.
In my iron sheet and board shack
I turn on the radio that lulls me to sleep . . .
But voices from America stir my soul and my nerves
and it is for me that Robeson and Marian sing
Negro spirituals from Harlem
Let my people go
Oh let my people go
let my people go
they say
and I open my eyes and I cannot sleep
inside me Anderson and Paul resound
not lullabies.
Let my people go.

Restlessly
I sit at the table to write
(deep inside me
oh let my people go)
let my people go
and now I am nothing but the instrument
of my swirling blood

Marian coming to my help
with her low voice, my sister.

I am writing
over my table familiar faces are bending
my mother with her rough hands and her face tired
with rebellions, pains, humiliations
tattooing in black the virgin white paper
and Paul that I do not know
but he is of the same blood and of the same beloved sap of
                                                    Mozambique
and miseries, wire-meshed windows, the goodbyes of magaiças
cottonfields and my unforgettable white friend
and Ze my brother and Paul
and you my friend with the gentle blue look
holding my hand and making me write
with gall flowing from our rebellion.
All come and bend over my shoulder
while I am writing, from the heart of the night
Marian and Paul watching from the radio light
let my people go
oh let my people go.

And as long as from Harlem reach me
these lamentations
and familiar faces visit me
on long sleepless nights
I shall not be distracted by the light music
of Strauss's waltzes
I shall write, I shall write
with Robeson and Marian by my side shouting
Let my people go
OH LET MY PEOPLE GO.

Translated from Mario de Andrade's French version by Jacques-Noël Gouat.

Jeni Couzyn

Morning

You are too naked for touching.
If I stroke your brown skin
as you sleep you may break. I irritate
your long dreams. I depress your awakening. I am
no good for you in your alien habitation.

Waiting for you to wake I wait
for a return from a long voyage, not knowing
what scurvy violence you bring back
to embarrass my clean house. Wherever I sow
perfection it grows into weeds. O my beautiful

How time changes the clean seed, how the corruption
of absence on my body, my damp hands. Awake
I am in sleep also, treacherous and lonely.
I don't know where to go, where to find rest.
Come back.

Spell for Jealousy

Be loved, my beloved.
Be sweetened, sour one.
Be filled, empty one.

Bring all the thief has given home to our house
Bring all the thief has given home to our bed
Bring all the thief has given home to our love
Bring all the thief has given home to me.

Light of her brighten me
Spite of her strengthen me
Joy of her gladden me.

Lady as candle is to the full sun of noon
As toad is to the great whale of the ocean
As leaf is to the mighty forest of the mountain
Are you now to me and my loved one.

Let the wind take you
Let the water take you
Let the rain take you

You are burr in his sock
You are grain in his shoe
Now he will forget you.

Spell to Protect our Love

By warm blood of bird
By wing of bird
By feather of bird
Let our love be safe.

By hot blood of mammal
By fur and by hair
By mammary gland
Let it come to no harm.

By chill blood of reptile
By scale of reptile
By lung of reptile
Let no ill damage it.

By four-legged amphibian
By gill and naked skin
By slow blood and lung
Adapt and be nourished.

By cool blood of fish
By gill and by fin
By scale and skeleton
Let no harm come to our love.

Spell to Cure Barrenness

Splinter under nail
  is the barren woman
Boil on the tongue
  is the childless woman
Abscess in the tooth
Thorn in the eye
Spite on the lips, O.

  Mind firm
  Heart open
  Earthquake waken

  Sperm speed
  Seed swell
  Womb be well
  Child be born
  Mourn no more.

Smell of the moor
Sound of the stream
Baby's cry in an old woman.

Spell for Birth

God the mother
God the daughter
God the holy spirit

Triune of love
Triune of grace

Stream take you
Current aid you
Earth receive you

God the mother
God the daughter
God the holy spirit

Triune of grace
Triune of power.

The Mystery

First I am one
then I am two
then I am one again
joined to she who was part of me
my love.
I am I
I am I and thee
I am I and she who was
I and thee
who kicks and strains in my belly
a trapped fish
she hammers on the doors of flesh
walls of the cave

a seed that sprouts arms and legs and eyes
a heart that suddenly begins
a beat of its own
a life that is my body
my cells my blood
that is also her body
her bones, her own skin and skeleton
her own heart
her own little hands
her two feet.
I am more than I
understand. As God creates the world
this is how it is for him:
eternally baffled, eternally
in love.

Heartsong

I heard your heartbeat.
It flew out into the room, a startled bird
whirring high and wild.

I stopped breathing to listen
so high and fast it would surely race itself
down and fall

but it held strong, light
vibrant beside the slow deep booming
my old heart suddenly audible.

Out of the union that holds us separate
you've sent me a sound like a name.
Now I know you'll be born.

Transformation

I see you dart into the world
pearly pink like the inside of a shell
streaked with silver.

Look! Look!
I am shouting with joy, rising up
like a phoenix from my pain

With my eyes I behold you
In the flesh I behold you

So a holy man waking into death
from a life of devotion or
martyrdom in flames

might look into the shining face of god
and see at once
he had never believed.

I see you with my eyes
I see you in my glory.

From the tatter of flesh I watch them work.
From a pinnacle of joy.
The placenta, purplish liver meat

sails out of my body like a whale
rubbery hands turn it inside out
hold it up to the light.

The sinewy pulsing cord.
In a haze of peace they cut and stitch
my threaded body like scarlet linen

the midwife chatting comfortably
seated at her work, the needle threaded,
the thimble, the green thread

in and out, in and out.
Then washed and trim in clean sheets
they leave us: mother father child

three folded together.
I see your sleeping face
eyelids crescent lines, lips curled translucent

in stillness like a cowrie shell
whirlpool of your hair. I see you breathe.
In a still pool the moon lies quiet.

The Pain

1

At first the pains crawl cautious in me
as thieving children.
I am holding my molecules in order with breathing

dream swimming on air I brace my power
concentrate on grace.
The afternoon unrolls its hoard of hours

contractions mounting like a tide
till rearing pains are white tipped breakers
hurling me up slamming me down

in swarming dark and I cry no more but it storms
wilder each moment
the lighted ward drowns in groundfog

I am lost
and pain is giant wheels of stone grinding me down
I am blind I am old

a croaking bird flies from my throat
the pain grinding me in its teeth
sweeps me out to sea

and a wellspring of rage breaks open in my tongue
but time has stopped
at twenty-five minutes past seven.

The hours writhe in the pain's mouth
clock a tormenting lamp in mist
on your wrist of glass I beg for release

I grip myself on
while the eagle in my cage of bone
drills talons deep.

Colours roar in my eyes
and voices reach me as voices reach out over waves
hold on breathe you are doing well

distant, meaningless and strange.
Day has slipped into night and night
drifts helpless towards dawn

when I rush into my senses again
words rolling at me like notes of a glass bell
one decent push and this baby would be born!

I am wild awake
teeth bared, a she wolf who turns from flight
snarling to face death

my voice releases and my muscles wrench
downwards into their final furious leap
to hurl you free

as you plunge into life.

2

Remembering this pain I feel myself betrayer
of a code we practice in the family of women
through generations.

When I see you
the pain in a moment races from memory
as the Tsunami that crushed the land

sweeps back to sea.
And I understand the lie my friends truthed me
before you were born:

Experience of a lifetime!
only the rush of joy when they see you
remembered.

We forget the pain.
We surrender the memory gladly, at once
hoarding no trace of bitterness or fear.

We'll have other children. Gaily
we encourage each other. Only our men
grey and shocked

whisper, huddle together
think themselves shameful cowards in their hearts
and pray with gratitude that they are men.

The Way Out

The way out is through fire,
a burning stairway
three doors like sentries.

The last but one
child from another time
steadies herself to brave it

then light and calm
darts into the burning.
Her courage cannot save her –

a haze of blue flames etch
their mad dance
that draws her like wind

waves of heat curl hissing
and scarlet break on her calves
she cries out with pain

as she passes through the first door
and labours upward
where soundless as the sun

the white fire
folds her to its breast.
Her breath sighs from her now

like dying leaves
as scorched and fainting she meets
the second door heavy as a vault

and passes through it
and climbs unfaltering
into the dark invisible heart of fire.

The last door
glows with angel heat, molten
immovable.

She flings her frail weight
against it
as it bites away her hands.

I remember a bird, nest aflame
its wings alight
circling higher and higher

into a black tar of smoke
like a beating star
circling and rising as its light

grew brighter and unbearably
brighter
towards a doorway that must open

a hand cool as rain .
outstretch
at the height of heaven.

The way out is never so bitter
never so bitter.
Perhaps it is through water.

Creation

You were made
under the sea
your ear gives you away.

You were made
in the calyx of a rose
your skin betrays you.

You were made in heaven
your eyelids as you sleep
cannot disguise themselves.

You were brought to me
by a giant kite
his wings stir white

on my face still.
Never say you grew
from a seed in my body

the dandelion brought you
the spring brought you
a star with brilliant hands

delivered you
leaving his light in your eyes
as a seal, and a promise.

Ingrid de Kok

Small Passing

For a woman whose baby died stillborn, and who was told by a man to stop mourning, 'for the trials and horrors suffered daily by black women in this country are more significant than the loss of one white child'.

1

In this country you may not
suffer the death of your stillborn,
remember the last push into shadow and silence,
the useless wires and cords on your stomach,
the nurse's face, the walls, the afterbirth in a basin.
Do not touch your breasts
still full of purpose.
Do not circle the house,
pack, unpack the small clothes.
Do not lie awake at night hearing
the doctor say 'It was just as well'
and 'You can have another.'
In this country you may not
mourn the small passings.

See: the newspaper boy in the rain
will sleep tonight in a doorway.
The woman in the busline
may next month be on a train
to a place not her own.
The baby in the backyard now
will be sent to a tired aunt,
grow chubby, then lean,
return a stranger.
Mandela's daughter tried to find her father
through the glass. She thought they would let her touch him.

And this woman's hands are so heavy when she dusts
the photographs of other children
they fall to the floor and break.
Clumsy woman, she moves so slowly
as if in a funeral rite.

On the pavements the nannies meet.
These are legal gatherings.
They talk about everything, about home,
while the children play among them,
their skins like litmus, their bonnets clean.

2

Small wrist in the grave.
Baby no one carried live
between houses, among trees.
Child shot running,
stones in his pocket,
boy's swollen stomach
full of hungry air.
Girls carrying babies
not much smaller than themselves.
Erosion. Soil washed down to the sea.

3

I think these mothers dream
headstones of the unborn.
Their mourning rises like a wall
no vine will cling to.
They will not tell you your suffering is white
They will not say it is just as well.
They will not compete for the ashes of infants.
I think they may say to you:
Come with us to the place of mothers.

We will stroke your flat empty belly,
let you weep with us in the dark,
and arm you with one of your babies
to carry home on your back.

Al Wat Kind Is

'They took all that was child in the house.'

(resident of Victoria West, reporting on police action in
the town)

They took all that was child
and in the dark closed room
visions of a ripe split melon
were at the tip of the knife
they held to the child's dry tongue.

All that was child
lies on the tarmac;
the intestines spill
like beans from a sack,
seaweed from the winter sea.

The bird of state has talons
and shit that drops like lead.
Its metal wings corrode the streets,
it hatches pools of blood.

A stone against a tank is a stone against a tank
but a bullet in a child's chest rips into the heart of the house.

But when in time the single stones
compact their weight and speed together,
roll up the incline towards the *lamvanger*'s lair,

crushing sand into rock, rock into boulder,
boulder into mountain, mountain into sky,
then the lungs of the bird will choke,
the wings will blister and crack,
at last the eyes will glaze, defeated.

And this torn light,
this long torn light
will repair itself
out of the filaments of children,
and all that is child will return to the house,
will return to the house.

Our Sharpeville

I was playing hopscotch on the slate
when the miners roared past in lorries,
their arms raised, signals at a crossing,
their chanting foreign and familiar,
like the call and answer of road gangs
across the veld, building hot arteries
from the heart of the Transvaal mine.

I ran to the gate to watch them pass.
And it seemed like a great caravan
moving across the desert to an oasis
I remembered from my Sunday-school book:
olive trees, a deep jade pool,
men resting in clusters after a long journey,
the danger of the mission still around them,
and night falling, its silver stars just like the ones
you got for remembering your Bible texts.

Then my grandmother called from behind the front door,
her voice a stiff broom over the steps:
'Come inside; they do things to little girls.'

For it was noon, and there was no jade pool.
Instead, a pool of blood that already had a living name
and grew like a shadow as the day lengthened.

The dead, buried in voices that reached even my gate,
the chanting men on the ambushed trucks,
these were not heroes in my town,
but maulers of children,
doing things that had to remain nameless.
And our Sharpeville was this fearful thing
that might tempt us across the well-swept streets.

If I had turned I would have seen
brocade curtains drawn tightly across sheer net ones,
known there were eyes behind both,
heard the dogs pacing the locked yard next door.
But, walking backwards, all I felt was shame,
at being a girl, at having been found at the gate,
at having heard my grandmother lie
and at the fear her lie might be true.
Walking backwards, called back,
I returned to the closed rooms, home.

Amelia Blossom Pegram

Mr White Discoverer

to cover your shame
you tied
my sunkissed breasts
tied
imprisoned
my swinging breasts
now
when
earthlight
merges into
my black body
then
phantom lover
you
come
unleash
my breasts
white feet
dancing
out of step
wrap
my legs
im
moral
ity
acts
sucks
my milk
But
Mr White
no blood
fevers

through my
untuned body
No more
no more
tonight's
last
moonkisses on breasts
tomorrow
my beads
tune
to sunkissed
swinging breasts

Mr White Discoverer
cover
your shame.

I will Still Sing

It is my celebration
I will drum my drum
I will sing my song
I will dance my dance
I do not need your anaemic hands
brought together in pale applause
I do not need your
'You are such musical people'
toothy smile
It is my celebration
You wonder what I have to celebrate
What does the drum tell me
If you must speculate
Watch out
One day as you throw your head back
As you gather your hearty laughter

I will change my dance
I will still sing
The drum will scream
Celebration.

Burials

dear God
i didn't kill the butterfly
i only buried it
in the foilwrapped matchbox
because
   i wanted it still to be pretty
for you
i sang one hymn
cried a little
i tended the grave
i found the dead sparrow
i buried it
in redcrepewrapped shoebox
'All things bright and beautiful'
i sang again
but
dear God
it's not because i loved burials
i don't need
five or ten daily
i don't know
what to sing
those children of Dimbaza had no time
to be bright and beautiful
i have run out of hymns
i cannot cry all day

Towards Abraham's Bosom

White cloth spread

Table Mountain
welcomes
All of no colour
to a banquet
While
on the sandy Cape Flats
Icy winds whip tattered clothes
cut through cracks
Empty bellies rumble
Frost-split feet shuffle
Huddled in plastic body bags
discarded
black bodies
wait
While
No Blacks feast
We wait
for the crumbs

Deliverance

Bear   down
My Mother Country
Push
You who have carried the seeds
full term
Bear   down
Push
Only you can give birth
to our freedom
Only you can feel the full

ripe weight
Bear   down
We will stand by you
We must relieve your pain
Bear   down   Bear down
Push

Ingrid Jonker

The Child who was Shot Dead by Soldiers at Nyanga

The child is not dead
the child lifts his fists against his mother
who shouts Afrika! shouts the breath
of freedom and the veld
in the locations of the cordoned heart

The child lifts his fists against his father
in the march of the generations
who shout Afrika! shout the breath
of righteousness and blood
in the streets of his embattled pride

The child is not dead
not at Langa nor at Nyanga
not at Orlando nor at Sharpeville
nor at the police station at Phillippi
where he lies with a bullet through his brain

The child is the dark shadow of the soldiers
on guard with rifles, saracens and batons
the child is present at all assemblies and law-givings
the child peers through the windows of houses and into the hearts
of mothers

this child who just wanted to play in the sun at Nyanga is
everywhere
the child grown to a man treks through all Africa
the child grown into a giant journeys through the whole world

Without a pass

I Don't Want Any More Visitors

I don't want any more visitors
not with cups of tea espresso and especially not brandy
I don't want to hear them waiting on winged letters
I don't want to hear them lying awake in their eyeballs while
the other sleeps wide like the horizon over his eyebrows
and what do I want to know about their same old ailments
the one without ovaries and the other with leukemia
the child without a music-box and the old man
who's now forgotten that he's deaf
the caprice of death in the robots of green
the people living by the sea as though in the Sahara
the betrayers of life with the face of death and of God

I want to be myself travelling with my loneliness
like a walking-stick
and believe I'm still unique

Translated from the Afrikaans by the poet

I Drift in the Wind

Free I have my own self-reliance
from graves and from deceptive friends
the hearth which I have cherished glares at me now
my parents have broken themselves off from my death
the worms stir against my mother my father
clasps his groping hand limp against the sky
free I believe my old friend has forsaken me
free I believe you have toppled the mountains in me
free my landscape smells of bitter sun and blood

What will become of me
the cornerstones of my heart bring no fulfilment
and my landscape is hardened in me
brooding and bitter but open

My nation
follow my lonely fingers
people be warm-hearted in yourselves
veiled in the sun of the coming days

My black Africa
follow my lonely fingers
follow my absent image
lonely as an owl

and the forsaken fingers of the world
alone like my sister
My people have rotted away from me
what will become of the rotten nation
a hand cannot pray alone.

The sun will cover us
the sun in our eyes forever covered
with black crows

Translated from the Afrikaans by Jack Cope

The Face of Love

Your face is the face of all the others
before you and after you and your eyes calm as a blue
dawn breaking time on time
herdsman of the clouds
sentinel of the white iridescent beauty
the landscape of your confessed mouth that I have explored

keeps the secret of a smile
like small white villages beyond the mountains
and your heartbeats the measure of their ecstasy

There is no question of beginning
there is no question of possession
there is no question of death
face of my beloved
the face of love

Translated from the Afrikaans by Jack Cope

I am With Those

I am with those
who abuse sex
because the individual doesn't count
with those who get drunk
against the abyss of the brain
against the illusion that life
once was good or had beauty or sense
against the garden parties of falsehood
against the silence that beats into the temples
with those who poor and old
race against death the atom-bomb of the days
and in shacks count the last
flies on the walls
with those stupefied in institutions
shocked with electric currents
through the cataracts of the senses
with those who have been deprived of their hearts
like the light out of the robot of safety
with those coloured, african dispossessed
with those who murder
because every death confirms anew
the lie of life

And please forget
about justice it doesn't exist
about brotherhood it's deceit
about love it has no right

Translated from the Afrikaans by Jack Cope and William Plomer

Pregnant Woman

I lie under the crust of the night singing,
curled up in the sewer, singing,
and my bloodchild lies in the water.

I play that I'm a child:
gooseberries, gooseberries and heather,
kukumakrankas, anise,
and the tadpole glides
in the slime in the stream
in my body
my foam-white image;
but sewer O sewer
my bloodchild lies in the water.

Still singing flesh-red our blood-song,
I and my yesterday
my yesterday hangs under my heart,
my wild lily, my lullaby world,
and my heart that sings like a cicada,
my cicada-heart sings like a cicada;
but sewer O sewer,
my bloodchild lies in the water.

I play that I'm happy:
look where the firefly sparkles!
the moon-disc, a wet snout that quivers –

but with the morning, the limping midwife,
grey and shivering on the sliding hills,
I push you out through the crust into daylight,
O sorrowing owl, great owl of the daylight
free from my womb but besmeared,
with my tears all smeared
and tainted with grief.

Sewer O sewer
I lie trembling, singing,
how else but trembling
with my bloodchild under your water. . . ?

Translated from the Afrikaans by Jack Cope and William Plomer

Dog

I lie under your hand – a cur
in the snarling silence
in the whimpering moon
trellised among the stars, she
in her terrifying
white coming and going.

(I too longed to go hunting hares
over my own karoo
over my burning plain
from ochre to ochre, oh
white plains of your hands!)

Tonight with my teeth bared I shall
jerk to the sly rhythm of the moon
listen to my sweetness and distance
my long-echoing bark
from my kennel white moon, white master
in the night.

Lindiwe Mabuza

A Love Song

It was good
The orchestral dance
Of our voices sipping dew
In the soft morning-rise
Of Africa south.
That was good.
We welcomed with a squeeze
The hand of desire as it dabbled and dappled
A summer mosaic
Across the canvas of thighs
Which swallowed the embrace
Of live dreams
It was good.

Now we swim in warm-baths
Of our nakedness,
Touching with our skin
The subterranean regions
Of our blood.
We move with the heave of time
Whose mouth is a fenceless water-fall
Stretching,
Turning some,
Now mellowing in one, with one.

It was good,
When tears watered the corpses
From the storage of past tales,
And tears circled their death
Above the face
Of the come of love

That was good.
Then we sponged
The ache of each beat
With the blend of hope
In sunbeam eyes
As I saw mine mirrored in yours.

February 1971

Dream Cloud

for my daughter, Thembilihle

Midnight wakes into noon
Noons break fast at night.
When it finally settles
This hovering womb of desire
Creation's pregnant cloud
Advances.
It whispers softly to the dream
As the dream entangles itself with strings
That stretch
To bounce sharp pins
And the dream rids sleep from its length
Making brief its own vision.
Desire moves –
The ancient infant of history enters then
Cracks
Our spent thought breathing
Writhing words into the silent wake
Of our movement
Itself pained by heavy
Back-breaking contraptions
Of false alarms
And other miscarriages of time

Bearing semblances of overdue relief
From long durations
And strangulations of strata.
At the chosen moment
(Which epochs never count
But the suns know it all)
Body sweat seethes gossamery threads from labour
Reaching skies that quiver with light
And the everlasting daughters of strength.
There she is, bundled
Fondness fondling this
Foundling of rain and earth
Growing to relay the burning torch
High into the gathering redness
Folding the day.

5 July 1976

Death to the Gold Mine!*

But there will be life.
Forever the reservoir will generate fresh chords
And the heirs will distil
The waters of white ridges!
And the heirs will distil
The deadly waters in the calcified bones in the ridges
From the classes of minerals in strata of stone
From eruptive lava
From volcanic layers of mountainous pressure
Clean rain on round pebbles
In our continuous stream
Of ripe blood.

*In September 1973, the South African police shot dead twelve striking mine workers at Carletonville Mine, near Johannesburg.

Tired Lizi Tired

Tru's god Lizi
I'm tired.
What?
What you say?
Ah! A letter from
My grandchild!

Lizi! It's summer over there!
They actually have earth
Like our soil she says.

America is burning!
Stores homes are burning she says!
Landlords shake insurance claims,
Black people just taking food
Clothes and anything brand new!
　　Heh?
　　What you say?
　　Makes no sense?
　　It's another world?

I wonder if she's tired already!
I hope she's not!
I hope she's . . .
　　Yes Ma'am!

Tru's god Lizi
I'm tired
Washing clothes for
Forty years!
Sure clothes and labels range
Sure fingers chafe and bleed
Yes
– but little white girls
don't never seem to change –

you are so nice mary
you are the best
laundry-girl mary!

Tru's god Lizi
I'm tired
Blowing these stubborn coals for
Slow winters!
Drains your body after a while
Cuts the heart cold! Lizi!
– then the complaints about
wrinkles creases and folds
   you are very careless mary.
   here, I have no use
   for such things!

Zindzi Mandela

I Have Tried Hard

I have tried hard
brother
and I won't give up
even if
that which I cannot see
creeps up behind me
and crushes me to pulp
or even if
that which I cannot see
overtakes me
and leaves me behind
to ponder

    conclude
I have yet to take
another step
and within that time
develop

I Waited for You Last Night

I waited for you last night
I lay there in my bed
like a plucked rose
its falling petals my tears

the sound that my room
   inhaled
   drew in softly
   swallowed
in my ears
was the tapping on the window

getting up
I opened it
and a moth flew in
powdering my neck
shrugging
I caught its tiny wings
and kissed it
I climbed back into bed
with it
and left it to flutter around my head

I waited for you last night

Saviour

An old woman standing
a young daughter opposite
both are waiting
in a wrinkled mind
   where are you Lord?
in a blossoming mind
   what are you Lord?
a white child running
a black child kneeling
both are young
in a polished mind
   a prayer tonight
in a deprived mind

   kneel all and sundry
an old man dying
a young son watching
both are pensive
in a dimming mind
   into your arms Lord
in a sorrowful mind
   release these chains

Lock the Place in your Heart

Lock the place in your heart
into which I have poured my emotions

I do not want to be hurt again
use your heartbeat as the key
only you can hear if it unlocks itself

If the wind around you
should blow away
breathe into it and let my secrets go

Gcina Mhlophe

Sometimes When It Rains

Sometimes when it rains
I smile to myself
And think of times when as a child
I'd sit by myself
And wonder why people need clothes

Sometimes when it rains
I think of times
when I'd run into the rain
Shouting 'Nkce – nkce mlanjana
When will I grow?
I'll grow up tomorrow!'

Sometimes when it rains
I think of times
When I watched goats
running so fast from the rain
While sheep seemed to enjoy it

Sometimes when it rains
I think of times
When we had to undress
Carry the small bundles of uniforms and books
On our heads
And cross the river after school

Sometimes when it rains
I remember times
When it would rain hard for hours
And fill our drum
so we didn't have to fetch water
From the river for a day or two

Sometimes when it rains
Rains for many hours without break
I think of people
who have nowhere to go
No home of their own
And no food to eat
Only rain water to drink

Sometimes when it rains
Rains for days without break
I think of mothers
Who give birth in squatter camps
Under plastic shelters
At the mercy of cold angry winds

Sometimes when it rains
I think of 'illegal' job seekers
in big cities
Dodging police vans in the rain
Hoping for darkness to come
So they can find some wet corner to hide in

Sometimes when it rains
Rains so hard hail joins in
I think of life prisoners
in all the jails of the world
And wonder if they still love
To see the rainbow at the end of the rain

Sometimes when it rains
With hail stones biting the grass
I can't help thinking they look like teeth
Many teeth of smiling friends
Then I wish that everyone else
Had something to smile about.

Phumzile Zulu

You are Mad: and I Mean It!

What did you mean when you called me benighted
Savage pagan barbarian
You must have been mad
I know now
I say it and I mean it

When you found me here in Africa
You said I was hungry
You came carrying a big book called 'BIBLE'
And you called yourself 'missionary'

You were going to offer
Food for my life
But to my surprise
Never was I hungry like this before

Instead of bread you gave crumbs
Maybe you just want me to salivate
Why do you act like this
Fat controlling experimenter
Who at the beginning called himself 'GOOD SAMARITAN'

I have realized that you did not mean all that good
You had come here to explore my wealth
Bloody spy in camouflage of a missionary
Did you think you would succeed forever and ever?

Look here . . .
Now that you are aware
That I am hard to get
You try and play monkey tricks
But you have failed with your BANTU EDUCATION
You thought I would bow down till when?

You stole my forefathers' land
You thought I would bow down till when? . . . Huh!
I mean it
And I mean it
I am not going to stand your lie
You found me comfortable
You requested that I give you fresh water and vegetables
And at the end my blood has become your water
My body your vegetables
I have given a hand
But now you want the whole arm
You are not going to get me
And I mean it!

You tell me you are going to give me scattered portions
Of my own soil
And now you claim that this is a whiteman's country
You forget how you came here
You are a fool
You are mad
And I mean it!

Kristina Rungano

Labour

For nine months I had borne him in my womb.
Nine months of disillusionment and pain
Relieved only occasionally by the gentle kicking within me;
The gentle movement of the life I created within me
Nine months I waited for this day;
Nine months and the grotesque lump growing on me.
And Kit always making numerous scarifices – of patience and
love –

Nine dreary months of waiting for this day.

And now I was beginning to feel sharp pains in me –
And mama saying they are labour pains –
The pains which will be the spring of new life . . .
Would it be a boy, I thought with intensified wonder,
– How proud his father would be,
– Or would it be a girl –
Someone I could teach to be just like me
And spoil with pretty frocks
And sweetly scented flowers to adorn her head?

I looked up into Kit's eyes
– The eyes that had seen me through
– The eyes that had known my sadness and joy for nine months
And saw in them all the love and care
– The pain which he felt for me
And like the sun on a cold morning
Relieved me of all fright, all desolation.

I looked with warm contemplation
To the moment when his warm embrace would say
'Our very own baby – the very essence of our love'
And tiny little hands would cling to my breasts in hunger

Tiny mouth drawing warm milk from me
An innocent little face looking into my face.
With trust
Learning me, just as Kit did.

I felt him, Kit
Captured by a foresight of summer days to come
The days when we – no longer just two –
Would walk in the dusk
Caressed by the warm breeze
And our child would learn to sing the birds to sleep
And dance the kan-kan with the fireflies.

And thus I was borne to the labour ward
Whilst Kit waited
– Waited again
– Waited in warm anticipation
– Waited for the awakening of my new beginning.

Mother

The thought of mother haunts my memory
Alone in her room, sobered by darkness
Her tears smelt of rotten flesh
Red eyes stared into the void
Shivering jewels of light that never blinked
Clouded so briefly by lucid images
of deep contemplation
and the sometimes stalwart shadow of gentility.
Thus she nursed her sorrow –
An archangel of stone –
Fighting the demons of despair.
It was never hard to recognize death's traces:
They hovered over her like hell's vultures
Now and again descending

Great pangs of pain unborn
Mother never screamed
Nor sob nor 'plaint.
She conquered yet never triumphed;
Her skin retained its sallow outlook.
She prayed in her silence
Deep cracks of white lips never moved
She appealed to the angels of the christian gospel
She called to her father and his fathers too:
But they never answered;
They never visited that dark room.
Then one day father came back
His spirit spoke through Imrai, his grandson
It called to us in the dark void
Then it spoke to my mother
Soft words we could not understand
A gentle whisper;
Mother's hands were raised
Calling to the waters of the sun for her soul
The spirit of my father cleansed her feet
Ululation and thanks to our great aunts
But father never came back again.

The Woman

A minute ago I came from the well
Where young women like myself drew water
My body was weary and my heart tired.
For a moment I watched the stream rush before me
And thought how fresh the smell of flowers,
How young the grass around it.
And yet again I heard the sound of duty
Which ground on me – made me feel aged
As I bore the great big clay container on my head
Like a great big painful umbrella.

Then I got home and cooked your meal
For you had been out drinking the pleasures of the flesh
While I toiled in the fields
Under the angry vigilance of the sun
A labour shared only by the bearings of my womb.
I washed your dishes
And swept the room we shared
Before I set forth to prepare your bedding
In the finest corner of the hut
Which was bathed by the sweet smell of dung
I had this morning applied to the floors.
Then you came in,
In your drunken lust
And you made your demands
When I explained how I was tired
And how I feared for your child in me
You beat me and had your way
At that moment
You left me unhappy and bitter
And I hated you;
Yet tomorrow I shall again wake up to you
Milk the cow, plough the land and cook your food,
You shall again be my Lord
For isn't it right that woman should obey,
Love, serve and honour her man?
For are you not fruit of the land?

This Morning

This morning I visited the place where we lay
like animals
O pride be forgotten
And how the moon bathed our savage nudity in purity
And your hands touched mine in a silken caress
And our beings were cleansed as though by wine.

Then you stroked my breast
And through love I shed the tears of my womb
O sweet fluid spilled in the name of love
O love
O sweet of mine existence
Your sigh of content as your lips touched my soul
O joy shared by the wilderness
O gentle breeze
O fireflies that hovered over our nest in protective harmony
How I yearn
I feel you here again with me.
See how the flowers, the grass, even the little shrubs have bloomed
Even as I bloomed under the warmth of your breath
And now they look at me; unashamed
For they have been washed and watered by the love of your loins
I stretch and sigh in warm contemplation
For tonight I shall again possess you
In me, I shall be content of all you render
On account of love
Under the stars I shall drink the whisperings of your body
Speak again to the depths of my sensibility
Tree of my life
Peaceful meadows
Cow dares not moo here
Ruler of the night
Lord dynamo
Let me not disturb your peace
But let me lie with you again
Be silent O silence
Love has found its awakening

After the Rain

The spots triumphed in the afternoon light;
There where the sun had at some time forgotten its duty
And somewhere higher up
The leaves bristled in the breeze
Devoid of shame they shook their bodies
And there where butterflies had perished
The soft raindrops had found a home
And about places where friend and foe had roamed
A gentle light seeped thro' from the white sky
And there the sorcerer's hand
For when it touched the flakes of water, they glistened
Till from afar they looked like virgin clouds
And one could almost feel their twinkle.

Yet no one dared look into the heavens
Nor learn that this was a time of silence
No bird, nor insect; grasshopper, mosquito, fly
Dared venture there where lightning had left its mark
Flocks of humanity had begun to fly from the roadsides
And for the moment serenity had captured its whoring wards
For whom peace would never be complete
And when finally the sun found courage
One was surprised to find that evening had so prematurely
                                                    descended
And it was too late to disturb the solitude which crept in
Tomorrow the trees'd look a day more ancient
Yet still it would be
The same familiar beautiful Zimbabwe.

BIOGRAPHICAL NOTES

Assumpta Acam-Oturu (Uganda) b. 15 August 1953 in Teso, Eastern Uganda. She obtained a Diploma in Journalism from Mindolo Ecumenical Centre's School of Journalism in Zambia and a BA in Journalism and International Relations from the University of Southern California (1983). She works for a radio station in Los Angeles. Her poems have appeared in *Ufahamu*.

Catherine Obianuju Acholonu (Nigeria) b. 26 October 1951 in Imo State. She was educated in Nigeria and at the University of Düsseldorf, in the former Federal Republic of Germany, where she obtained her MA and PhD. Since 1978 she has been a lecturer and Head of the English Department at Alvan Ikoku College of Education in Owerri, Nigeria. A prolific and widely published writer, her works include two volumes of poetry, *The Spring's Last Drop* (Totan Publishers, Owerri, 1985) and *Nigeria in the Year 1999* (Totan Publishers, Owerri, 1985), plays, primary school readers and critical studies of such writers as Buchi Emecheta and Christopher Okigbo. She is married with four children.

Ama Ata Aidoo (Ghana) b. 1942 at Abeadzi Kyiakor near Dominase, Central Ghana. After graduating with a BA from Legon, she studied Creative Writing at Stanford University, in California. She lectured at the University of Cape Coast and later served as Minister of Education in the Ghanaian government. Since the publication of her play, *The Dilemma of a Ghost* (Longman, Accra) in 1965, she has published *No Sweetness Here* (Longman, Harlow, 1969), *Anowa* (Longman, Harlow, 1970), *Our Sister Killjoy* (Longman, Harlow, 1973), *Someone Speaking to Sometime* (The College Press, Harare, 1985), *The Eagle and the Chickens and Other Stories* (1986) and *Changes* (The Women's Press, London, 1991). Her work appears in many international anthologies and journals. She lives in exile in Zimbabwe, with her daughter, Kinna.

Malak'Abd al-Aziz (Egypt) b. 1935; critic, poet and writer. At seventeen she published her first book, *Aghani al-Siba* (Songs of Youth). Other books include: *Qala al-Masa'* (The Night Narrated), 1966; *Bahr al-Samt* (Sea of Silence), 1969; *Ann Almisa Qalb al-Ahya'* (That I Touch the Heart of Things), 1974; and *Ughniyat li-l-Layl* (Songs of the Night), 1978. Some of her poems have been included in *The Longman Anthology of World Literature by Women: 1875–1975*.

Ifi Amadiume (Nigeria) currently lives and works in England. Her poems have appeared in *Okike*, *West Africa* and *Frontline* as well as in a number of other journals and anthologies. Her volume of poetry, *Passion Waves* (Karnak House, London, 1986) was a runner-up for the Commonwealth-British Airways Poetry Prize for 1986. She has also published *Male Daughters, Female Husbands* (Zed Press, London, 1987) a book about Igbo culture.

Danièle Amrane (Algeria). b. 1931 in Mọstaganem, her poems have appeared in Denise Barrat (ed.), *Espoir et parole: poèms algériens* (Seghers, Paris, 1964).

Irène Assiba d'Almeida (Benin). Educated in Benin, Nigeria, France and the USA, she has a BA (Licence d'Anglais), Université d'Amiens, France (1969), M.Phil. from the University of Ibadan, Nigeria (1979) and a PhD, Emory University, Atlanta, Georgia (1987). She collaborated with Olga Mahougbe on the translation of Chinua Achebe's *Arrow of God* into French as *La Flèche de Dieu* (Présence Africaine, Paris, 1978). She is currently translating Bernard Dadié's *Un nègre à Paris*, and teaching at the University of Arizona, Phoenix.

Abena P. A. Busia (Ghana) b. 1953, is the daughter of the late Dr Kofi Busia, former Prime Minister of Ghana. Educated in Ghana, Holland, Mexico and England, she holds a BA (1976), an MA (1980) and a D. Phil. (1984) from Oxford University. She has published *Testimonies of Exile* (Africa World Press, New Jersey, 1990). Some of her poems have been included in *Summer Fires: New Poetry from Africa* (Heinemann, Oxford, 1983).

Gladys May Casely Hayford (alias Aquah Laluah) (Ghana) b. 11 May 1904 at Axim, Ghana. She studied in Wales, danced with a jazz band in Berlin, then became a teacher in her mother's Girls' Vocational School in Freetown, Sierra Leone. Her earliest poems appeared in the *Atlantic Monthly* magazine, *The Philadelphia Tribune* and other journals. Some of her poems are included in the following anthologies: Countee Cullen's *Caroling Dusk: An Anthology of Verse by Negro Poets* (1927); Langstone Hughes' *Poetry of the Negro World* (1949); the *African Treasury* (1960) and *Poems from Black Africa* (1963) as well as in Langstone Hughes and Christiane Reynault (eds), *Antologie Africaine et Malgache* (1962). She died in October 1950 in Freetown, Sierra Leone.

Andrée Chedid (Egypt) b. 1921, of Egyptian-Lebanese parents, in Cairo. She has lived in Paris since the age of twenty-one, except for short periods of study in Egypt for a BA and in Lebanon. She has published twenty-two volumes of poems, seven novels, five plays and other writings, and has won many major literary awards.

Jeni Couzyn (South Africa) b. 1942. Educated in South Africa, she moved first to England, then to Victoria, British Columbia, and settled for a time in Toronto, Ontario. She currently lives in London. Her poems have been published in South African, British and Canadian journals. She has published the following volumes of poetry: *Flying* (Workshop Press, London, 1970); *Monkey Wedding* (Jonathan Cape, London, 1972); *Christmas in Africa* (Heinemann, London, 1975); *House of Changes* (Heinemann, London, 1978); *The Happiness Bird* (Sono Nis Press, Toronto, 1978); and *Life by Drowning* (House of Anansi Press, Toronto, 1983). She is also the editor of *The Bloodaxe Book of Contemporary Women Poets* (Bloodaxe, Newcastle upon Tyne, 1985).

Ingrid de Kok (South Africa) b. 1951. She obtained a BA in Politics and English from the University of Witwatersrand, an honours degree from the University of Cape Town, and an MA in English Literature from Queens University, Canada. She has published a book of poems, *Familiar Ground* (Ravan Press, Johannesburg, 1989).

Noémia de Sousa (Mozambique) b. 20 September 1927, in Maputo, and educated in Mozambique, Brazil and Portugal. Between 1951 and 1964 she worked on various Angolan and Mozambican journals, and published her poetry in Angolan, Mozambican, Brazilian, Portuguese and French reviews. Among the foremost Mozambican Negritude poets, de Sousa was the *first* African woman to gain an international reputation as a poet, and she greatly influenced later generations of Mozambican poets. She fled into exile in France during the Mozambican liberation war, in the late 1960s, married a Portuguese man and stopped writing poetry for a while. After the war, she returned briefly to Mozambique, but went back to Europe. Her poems have appeared in Mario de Andrade's *Caderno de poesia negra de expressão portuguêsa* (Livraria Escolar Editora, Lisbon, 1953), *The Penguin Book of Modern African Poetry*, *The Penguin Book of Women Poets*, *Women Poets of the World* (Macmillan, New York, 1983), *The Other Voice: Twentieth Century Women's Poetry in Translation* (Norton, New York, 1976), *Sunflower of Hope: Poems from the Mozambican Revolution* and Frank Chipasula's *When My Brothers Come Home: Poems from Central and Southern Africa* (Wesleyan University Press, Middletown, Connecticut, 1985).

Leila Djabali (Algeria) b. 1933, was among the young intellectuals imprisoned by the French colonial authorities for her part in the Algerian liberation struggle. Her poem, 'For my Torturer, Lieutenant D . . .', which vividly recreates her prison ordeal, first appeared in Joana Bankier and Deirdrie Lashgari (eds), *Women Poets of the World* (Macmillan, New York, 1983).

Alda do Espirito Santo (São Tomé e Príncipe) b. 30 April 1926; coloured. After her studies in Portugal, she returned to São Tomé where she was a primary school teacher. She collaborated on *Mensagem*, *Imbondeiro* and other Angolan and Mozambican journals. Her poems are included in Mario de Andrade's *Caderno: Poesia negra de expressão portuguêsa* (Casa des Estudantes do Império,

Lisbon, 1953), *Antologia de poesia negra de expressão portuguêsa* (Paris, 1953), *Estrada larga* (Porto, s/d 1962), *Europe-Revue mansuelle*, Vol. 39, No. 381 (Paris, January 1962), *Poetas de São Tomé e Príncipe* (Lisbon, 1963), *Nova soma de poesia do mundo negro* (Présence Africaine, Paris, 1966), *Poetas e Contistas Africanos de expressão portuguêsa (Editora Brasiliense, 1963)*, *Literatura africana de expressão portuguêsa*, Vol. 1, *Poesia* (Argel, 1967), *La poésie africaine d'expression portugaise* (Paris, 1969), *Contos portuguêses do ultrama*, Vol. 1 (Porto, 1969), *Afrikansk lyrik* (Sueca, Stockholm, 1970), *No Reino de Caliban* (Seara Nova, Lisbon, 1976), and *Antologia tematica de poesia africana* (Lisbon, 1976). She is a member of the Political Bureau of the Movement for the Liberation of São Tomé e Príncipe (MLSTP) and Minister of Education and Culture in the government of the Democratic Republic of São Tomé e Príncipe.

Marina Gashe (Mrs Elimo Njau) (Kenya); teacher, playwright and poet who studied at Makerere University College, Kampala, Uganda. In 1960, her first play, *The Scar*, won a drama festival award at the National Theatre in Kampala. She is married to the famous Tanzanian painter, Elimo Njau, a Chako from the slopes of Mt Kilimanjaro.

Anna Gréki (Algeria) 1931–1966, was among the young women intellectuals who were detained, tortured and exiled by the French colonial authorities during the Algerian freedom struggle. She published a bilingual French-Arabic volume of poems, *Algérie, capital Alger* (SNED, Tunis, 1963), followed by *Temps fort* (Présence Africaine, Paris, 1966). Other poems appear in Denise Barrat (ed.), *Espoir et paroles: poèmes algériens* (Seghers, Paris, 1964), and *Women Poets of the World* (Macmillan, New York, 1983). 'Anna Gréki' is the pseudonym of Colette Anne Gregoire.

Queen Hatshepsut (Egypt), daughter of Thutmose I and widow of her own brother, Thutmose II, ruled and dressed as a male pharaoh during the Eighteenth Dynasty as a regent for Thutmose III for two years but crowned herself king in order to normalise her rule, claiming Amun Re, the Sun God, as her father. The strongest of the five female Pharaohs in Egyptian history, Hatshepsut referred to herself as both male and female, 'son' and 'daughter'. She built a huge mortuary temple at Deir el Bahari, in the mountains. Of the giant granite obelisks that she erected in the temple of Amun Re at Karnak, only two survive.

Shakuntala Hawoldar (Mauritius) b. 15 September 1944 in Bombay, India. In 1967 she emigrated to Mauritius and married a Mauritian. She has three children. She worked in the Audio-Visual Section of the Ministry of Education and Culture. Her poetry is collected in *I've Seen Strange Things* (Mauritius Printing Co., Port Louis, 1971), *Moods, Moments and Memories* (The Triveni, Beau Bassin, 1972) and *You* (Lemwee Graphics, Beau Bois-St Pierre, 1981). Although Ms Hawoldar currently lives in India, following her divorce, her poetry remains an intimate part of her Mauritian experience.

Rashidah Ismaili (Nigeria) b. 12 July 1941 in Cotonou, Benin. First educated in a Quranic school developed and headed by her maternal grandmother, she went to France and Italy to elude her Nigerian father's attempt to marry her off. Later she chose her own husband, studied for a BA in Music (Voice) at the New York College of Music, and obtained an MA in Social Psychology and a PhD in Psychology from the New School for Social Research, New York. Her volumes of poetry are *Oniybo and Other Poems* (Shamal Books, New York, 1985), and *Missing in Action and Presumed Dead* (Africa World Press, New Jersey, 1992). She is represented in Amiri and Amina Baraka's anthology, *Confirmations* (William Morrow, New York, 1983) and *Womanrise* (Shamal Books, New York, 1978). She lives in Harlem but teaches at Rutgers University in New Jersey. She is a divorced mother of a grown-up son, Daoud Samir.

Ingrid Jonker (South Africa) 1933–1965; began writing poetry as a child, and at sixteen she submitted her first manuscript to a publisher, but it was rejected. In 1956 she published *Ontvlugting* (Escape) (Uitgewery Culemborg, Cape Town, 1956), followed in

1963 by her prize-winning *Rook en Oker* (Smoke and Ochre) (Afrikaanse Pers-Boekhandel, Johannesburg 1963), which established her as one of the most brilliant and original South African poets. In July 1965 she committed suicide as a result of her estrangement from her father, Abraham Jonker, a prominent newspaper editor and Nationalist Party official. In 1966, her friends Jack Cope and William Plomer published a posthumous volume of her poems entitled *Kantelson* (Setting Sun) (Afrikaanse Pers-Boekhandel, Johannesburg, 1966). In further recognition of her contribution to South African letters, they assembled the English versions of her poems which she had prepared, into *Selected Poems* (Jonathan Cape, London, 1968). Other works include *The Goat and Other Stories*, and a play, *A Son After My Heart*. Her poems appear in numerous anthologies such as *The Other Voice: Twentieth Century Women's Poetry in Translation* (Norton, New York, 1976), *The Penguin Book of Women Poets*, *The Penguin Book of Southern African Verse*, and *The Longman Anthology of World Literature by Women: 1875–1975*. Most of her writings were published in her *Collected Works* (1975).

Gwendoline C. Konie (Zambia). Once Zambia's ambassador to the United Nations, she is currently a business woman in Lusaka, where she runs Copatan Enterprises and edits and publishes *Woman's Exclusive*, the country's first ever magazine devoted exclusively to women's issues.

Alda Lara (Alda Ferriera Pires Barreto de Lara Albuquerque) (Angola) b. 6 September 1930, Benguela; d. 30 January 1962, Cambambe; white, physician trained at the School of Medicine of the universities of Lisbon and Coimbra, Portugal, where she was active in the Casa dos Estudantes do Império (CEI), together with other African poets. Following her death, the Camara Municipality of the City of Sá da Bandeira instituted the Alda Lara Prize for Poetry. Her husband, the writer Orlando Albuquerque, edited and published her posthumous volume of poetry and a collection of short stories. Her work appears in *Mensagem, Antologia de poesia angolanos* (Nova Lisboa, 1958), *Estudos Ultramarinos*, No. 3 (Lisbon,

1959), *Antologia de terra portuguêsa – Angola* (Lisbon), *Poesia angolanos* (Lisbon, 1962), *Poetas e contistas africanos* (São Paulo, 1963), *Mákua 2–antologia poetica* (Sá da Bandeira, 1963), *Mákua 3* (Sá da Bandeira, 1963), *Antologia poética angolana* (Sá da Bandeira, 1963), *Contos portuguêses do ultramar – Angola*, Vol. 2 (Porto, 1969) and *No Reino de Caliban* (Seara Nova, Lisbon, 1976). Her posthumous books are *Poemas* (Ediçoes Imbondeiro, Sá da Bandeira, 1966) and *Tempo de Chuva* (Lobito, 1973).

Maria Eugénia Lima (Maria Eugénia Pimentel Lima Silva) (Angola) b. 22 October 1935; coloured. Educated in Angola and Portugal, her writings have been published in Portuguese and Angolan newspapers and journals. In 1964 she published *Entre a pantera e o espelho* (Tipografia Nunes, Porto, 1964), *Binómio do sangue* (poems) and *A Cidade às escuras*, a play set in Angola in the late nineteenth century. She is represented in Manuel Ferreira's *No Reino de Caliban* (Seara Nova, Lisbon, 1976).

Lindiwe Mabuza (South Africa) b. 1938 in Newcastle, Natal Province. She obtained a BA from the University of Botswana, Lesotho and Swaziland, Roma; an MA in American Studies (1968) from the University of Minnesota, and another in Literature from Stanford University. She has taught at Ohio University and the University of Minnesota. Her poems have appeared in South African and American journals. Selections of her work have been published in Anta Sudan Katara Mberi and Cosmo Pieterse (eds), *Speak Easy, Speak Free* (International Publishers, New York, 1977), Barry Feinberg (ed.), *Poets to the People* (Heinemann Educational Books, London, 1980) and *Malibongwe*. Her collection of poems, *Letter to Letta* was published by Skotaville Publishers, Johannesburg, in 1991. She has been an ANC Representative to the USA.

Rachida Madani (Morocco) b. 1953 in Tangier. In 1981 she published her volume of poems, *Femme je suis* (Ineditions Barbare, Vitry, 1981). She currently lives in Tangier.

Zindzi Mandela (South Africa), daughter of Winnie and Nelson

Mandela. As a teenager she published two volumes of poetry, *Black As I Am* (Guild of Tutors Press, Los Angeles, 1978) and *Black and Fourteen*. Some of her poems have appeared in such anthologies as *If You Want to Know Me* (Friendship Press, New York, 1978) and Frank Chipasula's *When My Brothers Come Home: Poems from Central and Southern Africa* (Wesleyan University Press, Middletown, Connecticut, 1985).

Joyce Mansour (Egypt) b. 1928 in London, England. After a brief stay in Egypt she lived in Paris where she was a leading member of the contemporary surrealist movement until her death in 1986. Her poetry books include *Rapaces* (Seghers, Paris, 1960), *Carré Blanc* (Soleil Noir, Paris, 1965) *Phallus et momies* (Daily-Bul, Paris, 1969), *Jasmin d'hiver* (Fata Margana, Paris, 1982), *Flammes immobiles* (Fata Margana, Paris, 1986) and *Prose & Poésie: Oeuvre Complète* (Actes Sud, Arles, 1991). A widely anthologised poet, she appears in *The Penguin Book of Women Poets* and *Women Poets of the World from Antiquity to Now*.

Maria Manuela Margarido (São Tomé e Príncipe) b. 9 November 1925 at Roça Olímpia on Príncipe Island; coloured. She studied film and theology in Lisbon where she was a participant in the students' cultural programs in the Casa dos Estudantes do Império (CEI). Arrested by the Policia Internacional de Defesa do Estado (PIDE) in 1962, she has since lived in Paris, working for the Secretariat-Library of the Institute of Portuguese and Brazilian Studies at the Sorbonne. In 1957 she published *Alto como o silêncio* (Publicacoes Europa-America, Lisboa, 1957), a book of poems. Her poems have been published in such reviews and anthologies as *Mensagem* (CEI, Lisbon), *Estudos Ultramarinas* (Lisbon, 1969), *Poetas de São Tomé e Príncipe* (CEI, Lisbon, 1963), *Poetas e contistas africanos* (São Paulo, 1963), *Nova soma de poesia do mundo negro* (Présence Africaine, No 57, Paris, 1966) and *Women Poets of the World*.

Annette M'Baye d'Erneville (Senegal) b. 1927; Sokhone. An important radio personality, journalist, cultural activist, and cofounder and editor-in-chief of *Awa: Revue de la femme noire*, her poems have been collected in two chapbooks, *Poèmes africaines* (Centre d'Art National Français, Paris-Toulouse, 1965), which was awarded the Prix des Poètes Sénégalais de Langue Française in 1964 when in manuscript form, and *Kadda* (Imprimerie Diop, Dakar, 1966). She is represented in *Nouvelle somme de la poésie du monde noir* (Présence Africaine, Paris, 1966), Norman Shapiro (ed.), *Negritude: Black Poetry from Africa and the Caribbean* (October House, Stonington, Connecticut, 1970), G. Bonn (ed.), *Le Sénégal écrit* (H. Erdmann, Tubingen, and Nouvelles Editions Africaines, Dakar, 1980) and in *Women Poets of the World*. She has also published poems and stories for children.

Gcina Mhlophe (South Africa) born Nokugcina ('the last one') in 1959 in Hammarsdale. She used a public toilet in a Johannesburg park, during recess from her factory job, to write. A well-known actress at the Market Theatre, she has also acted at the Edinburgh Festival, and toured Britain, Europe, and the USA. She plays a leading role in the film, *A Place of Weeping*, and she has acted in the following plays: *The Nurse* (1982); *Black Dog, Born in the RSA*, for which she won an Obie Award (published in *Woza Afrika: An Anthology of South African Plays*. George Braziller, New York, 1986), and her own, *Have You Seen Zandile?* She is anthologised in *Sometimes When It Rains* (Pandora Press, London, 1987), *Spare Rib* and *A Land Apart* (Faber & Faber, London/Viking Penguin, New York, 1987).

Mwana Kupona binti Msham (Kenya) *c.*1810–*c.*1860; pioneer nineteenth-century Swahili poet from Pate Island. Widow of Sheikh Mataka ibn Mbaraka (1779–1856), a famous personality in Swahili political history, who conducted guerrilla warfare against Saiyid Said, the Sultan of Zanzibar. Mwana Kupona had two children by Mataka, a boy, Muhammad bin Sheikh, and a girl, Mwana Hashima binti Sheikh, for whom in 1858, in anticipation of her own death, she wrote her famous 'Poem of Mwana Kupona' for her daughter's social edification.

Micere Githae Mugo (Kenya); poet, critic and playwright. After her education in Canada, she lectured at Nairobi University until her detention by the Kenyan government. After her release, she went into exile in Zimbabwe where she lectures at the University of Zimbabwe. Her volume of poems, *Daughter of My People, Sing* (Kenya Literature Bureau, Nairobi, 1976) has been literally 'detained' since her own imprisonment. She published a play, *The Long Illness of Ex-Chief Kiti* (1976) and collaborated with Ngũgĩ wa Thiong'o on the play, *The Trial of Dedan Kimathi* (Heinemann, Oxford, 1976). In 1978 she published *Visions of Africa*, a critical study.

Malika O'Lahsen (Algeria) b. 1930 in Algiers, her poems have been included in *Espoir et paroles: poèmes algériens* (Seghers, Paris, 1964).

Molara Ogundipe-Leslie (Nigeria) b. 1941, was educated at Ibadan University where she has also been a Senior Lecturer. A well-known literary critic, she has published a book of poems, *Sew the Old Days and Other Poems* (Evans Brothers, Ibadan, 1985) and has been anthologised in *The Penguin Book of Modern African Verse* (1984). She was Head of the English Department at Ogun State University, Nigeria but she is currently Director of the Women's Studies Program at Indiana University – Perdue University in Fort Wayne, Indiana, USA.

Marjorie Oludhe Macgoye (Kenya) b. 1928 in England, obtained an MA from the University of London, and went to Kenya where she married and became a Kenyan citizen at Independence. A retired missionary bookseller, she has been widely published in East African and British journals as well as such anthologies as *Introduction to East African Poetry, Summer Fires: New Poetry of Africa* (Heinemann, London, 1983), *Boundless Voices* and *The Heinemann Book of African Poetry in English* (1990). Her novels include *Growing up at Lina School* (OUP, 1971), *Murder in Majengo* (OUP, 1972), and *Coming to Birth* (Virago, London, 1986), winner of the Sinclair Award for Fiction. She has also published *Song of Nyarloka and Other Poems* (OUP, Nairobi, 1977), *The Story of*

Kenya (1986), *The Present Moment* (1987) and *Street Life* (novella, 1987). She won third prize in the 1981 BBC Arts and Africa Poetry Competition. She has four grown-up children, and currently lives in Nairobi.

Amelia Blossom Pegram (South Africa) born in Cape Town. She was trained as a teacher at Hewat Training College, and later studied at the University of Cape Town, the Guildhall School of Music and Drama in London, and the University of Louisville, Kentucky. She is widely published and translated. Her books are *Deliverance: Poems for South Africa* (a self-published chapbook) and *Our Sun Will Rise* (Three Continents Press, Washington, DC, 1989).

Kristina Rungano (Zimbabwe) b. 28 February 1963. After obtaining a Diploma in Computer Science in Britain, she returned to work for the Science Computing Centre in Harare. She has published a volume of her poems, *A Storm is Brewing* (Zimbabwe Publishing House, Harare, 1984).

Amina Saïd (Tunisia) b. 1953 in Tunis. Her books of poetry include *Paysages, nuit friable* (1980) and *Métamorphose et la vague* (1985).

Amélia Veiga (Amélia Maria Ramos Veiga Silva) (Angola) b. 1 December 1931 at Silves, Portugal. In 1951 she emigrated to Angola where she taught in the commercial institutes of Sá da Bandeira. In 1962, the city's Camara Municipality awarded her the Fernando Pessoa Prize for her book, *Poemas* and the first Jogos Florais Prize. She contributed to Angolan, Portuguese and Brazilian journals. Her poems appear in *Mákua 1 – antologia poética* (Sá da Bandeira, 1962), *Mákua 3 – antologia poética* (Sá da Bandeira, 1963), and *O corpo da Pátria (antologia poética da guerra no ultramar 1961/1971*, (Braga, 1971). Her published books are *Destinos* (Sá da Bandeira, 1961), *Poemas* (Sá da Bandeira, 1963) and *Libertação* (Sá da Bandeira, 1974).

Phumzile Zulu (South Africa). In 1978 she went into exile in the USA, where she enrolled in New York University as the first recipient of the Bishop Tutu Scholarship. Her poetry has appeared in Sono Molefe's *Malibongwe ANC Women: Poetry is also their Weapon* (ANC, Stockholm, 1981) and in *IKON: Art Against Apartheid* (second series 5/6, Winter/Summer 1986).

ACKNOWLEDGEMENTS

THE HEINEMANN BOOK OF AFRICAN WOMEN'S POETRY

edited by

Frank and Stella Chipasula

The editors and publishers wish to thank the following for permission to use copyright material:

Irène Assiba d'Almeida for her poem, 'Sister, You Cannot Think a Baby Out'; Anita Barrows for her translations of Anna Greki, 'Before Your Waking and Leila Djabali, 'For My Torturer, Lieutenant . . .' from *Women Poets of the World*, 1983, Macmillan Inc.; Cherry Valley Editions for Joyce Mansour, 'Of Sweet Rest', 'Desire as Light as a Shuttle' and 'A Woman Kneeling in the Sorry Jelly' from *Flash Card*, translated by Mary Beach, 1978; College Press Publishers (Pvt) Ltd., Zimbabwe, for Ama Ata Aidoo, 'Gynae One', Issues', 'For Kinna II' and 'Totems' from *Someone Talking to Sometime*, 1985; Flammarion for Andrée Chedid, 'What Are We Playing At?', 'Imagine', 'Who Remains Standing?' and 'The Naked Face' from *Contre chant*, 1968: Andrée Chedid, 'For Survival' and 'Setting Aside' from *Visage premier*, 1972; and Andrée Chedid, 'Future and The Ancestor', 'Movement' and 'Man-Today' from *Fraternité de la parole*, 1976; Jacques-Noël Gouat for the translation rights in Noémia de Sousa, 'Call', 'Our Voice' and 'Let My People Go', and Alda do Espirito Santo, 'Where are the Men Chased Away by that Mad Wind?', 'Grandma Mariana' and 'Far from the Beach'; Shakuntala Hawoldar for her poems, 'To Be a Woman', 'The Woman', 'You', 'Destruction', 'You Have Touched My Skin', 'You Must Help Me Gather', 'I Am Not Just A Body For You', 'Beyond Poetry', 'It Is Not Just', 'To my Little Girl' and 'I Have Gone Into My Prison Cell'; Rashidah Ismaili for her poems, 'Bajji', 'Solange', 'Lagos', 'Queue' and 'Yet Still' from *Oniybo & Other Poems*, Shamal Books, Inc., 1985; Karnak House for Ifi Amadiume, 'Nok Lady in Terracotta', 'The Union', 'We Have Even Lost Our Tongues', 'Creation' and 'Be Brothers' from *Passion Waves*. Copyright © 1985 Karnak House; Marjorie Oludhe Macgoye for her poems, 'For Miriam', 'A Freedom Song', 'Letter to a Friend' and 'A Muffled Cry: For Chelagat Mutai' from *Song of Nyarloka and Other Poems*, Oxford University Press, 1977; Andrew Mann Ltd. on behalf of the author for Jeni Couzyn, 'The Mystery', 'Transformation', 'The Pain' and 'Spell for Jealousy' from *Life By Drowning*, 1982, House of Anansi Press; and 'Morning', 'Spell To Protect Our Love', 'Spell to Cure Barrenness', 'Spell for Birth', 'Heartsong', 'The Way Out' and 'Creation' from *Monkey's Wedding*, 1972, Jonathan Cape; Mildred P.